COUNTRY INNS
OF THE
MID-ATLANTIC

To: Grandmom & Grandpop.

Thought you may enjoy this.

Love,

Vonrie

COUNTRY INNS
OF THE
MID-ATLANTIC

ROBERT W. TOLF

ROY KILLEEN
Illustrations

101 PRODUCTIONS
San Francisco

COVER ILLUSTRATION: CAPTAIN MEY'S INN, Cape May, New Jersey
Illustration by Roy Killeen. Color Rendering by Sara Raffetto.

MAPS: Lynne O'Neil

Some of the drawings in this book have been reproduced from the inns' brochures, with permission of the inns, and are credited to the following artists or sources: The Chalfonte, page 13; The Duke of Windsor Inn, page 15, Marsha Cudworth; The Mainstay, page 17, Edith Hewitt; Victorian Rose, page 21, Edith Hewitt; Publick House, page 27, Judi Goldwasser-Petrini; The Sign of the Sorrel Horse, page 39; Black Bass Hotel, page 44; The Wedgewood Inn, page 50, Carol Stoddard; Barley Sheaf Farm, page 52, Linda Hall; Longwood Inn, page 58; Duling Kurtz House and Country Inn, page 60; The Overlook Inn, page 66; Settler's Inn, page 69, Pat Baker; Victorian Inn, page 76, Barb Mower; Tulpehocken Manor Inn and Plantation, page 84, Bill Cohlmohn; Historic 1725 Witmer's Tavern, page 87, Brant E. Hartung; Strasburg Village Inn, page 93, David Sabella; General Sutter Inn, page 94; The Spring House, page 99, John Suplee; Allenberry Resort Inn and Playhouse, page 101; Kane Manor Country Inn, page 108, Denny Driscoll; Century Inn, page 112; Casselman Inn, page 116, Marie Guard; Bed and Board at Tran Crossing, page 125, Linda Lubensky; The Rosebud Inn, page 126, Helen Smith; The Inn at Buckeystown, page 128, Marilu Tousignaut; The Strawberry Inn, page 130, Ruth Anderson; Gibson's Lodgings, page 135, Tom Ellison; The Tidewater Inn, page 142, John Moll; Harrison's Chesapeake House, page 148; Robert Morris Inn, page 152, John Moll; The Corner Cupboard Inn, page 162, Lois Wood; The Pleasant Inn, page 166, Dan Costan.

Printed and bound in the United States of America.
Distributed to the book trade in the United States
by the Macmillan Publishing Company, New York.

Published by 101 Productions
834 Mission Street
San Francisco, California 94103

Library of Congress Cataloging-in-Publication Data

Tolf, Robert W.
    Country inns of the Mid-Atlantic.

    Includes index.
    1. Hotels, taverns, etc.--Pennsylvania--Directories.
2. Hotels, taverns, etc.--Maryland--Directories.
3. Hotels, taverns, etc.--New Jersey--Directories.
I. Title.
TX907.T5329 1986   647'.9475'01   86-1432
ISBN 0-89286-234-3

CONTENTS

INTRODUCTION

In a lifetime of travel and adventure I've made a practice of collecting special overnighting experiences in this country and abroad. When the inn craze hit its stride, I finally started putting that experience to good use, writing columns and articles on innings good and bad in the U.S.

In 1979 I collated the collected material covering the dozen states of the Confederacy and came out with *Country Inns of the Old South,* my first inns book. That was followed by a totally revised and greatly expanded version four years later (with 164 inns instead of the original 62) and in January 1985, *Country Inns of New York State* was released, describing 120 special experiences in the Empire State.

That book reflected many memories from living there plus up-to-date surveys and seemingly endless reconnaisance tours which took me from one end of the state to the other—several times. Although distant from my own southern turf, the land gave me welcome opportunities to revisit old friends—not people, but cities, museums, art galleries, main streets, historic monuments, lakes, mountains, streams—and find new ones: inns worthy to be included in a guidebook based on personal inspection.

I suppose it was inevitable that I would bridge the gap between New York and the Old South by crossing the several borders and driving through countryside and alongside ocean bays every bit as dramatic and captivating as any I've encountered anywhere in the world. I was, after all, merely going home, having lived in the Mid-Atlantic area off and on for fifteen years. I was returning to the tranquil shores of the Chesapeake, rediscovering the restful retreats close to and sometimes within the crowded cities of the eastern corridor, or escaping to the Poconos when they were blanketed with snow and speckled with skiers, to Pennsylvania Dutch country for the fall harvest, the Welsh Mountains and Brandywine Valley for the arrival of spring, and the Victorian jewel collection of Cape May for the celebration of Christmas.

Everywhere in the mid-Atlantic, from the western marches of Pennsylvania and the mountains of Maryland all the way to the Jersey shore, I had my special "innings"—experiences that were acres and sometimes centuries removed from the routine of shag carpeting, sterile staffs, never-ending corridors and canyons of look-alike rooms. Everywhere I went—and I traveled thousands of miles in my quest— I found abiding relief from the mediocrity and monotony of Samesville, USA. I found the very definitions of those much-abused and over-used words—"quaint," "picturesque" and "charming"—as I collected the inns for inclusion in this book and rejected others which did not meet the mark.

Which made the final cut? Those hostelries regardless of size, cost or location which were in one or several ways exemplary. In setting, in the sense of place and history, in the extra-step amenities, the personalized concern, the level of enchantment and degree of "innovative" committment to the comfort of their passing parade of guests.

No one pays to get a mention in this book—or anything else I've written on inns, restaurants and travel destinations. No inn is required to buy a set number of books for resale or to join some kind of association as the price of admission to these pages. The search for the best, the decision to include or not, is strictly mine, made after careful consideration of all the factors, and only after personal inspection and on-scene surveys. I visit the inns—all of them—sometimes with trumpets blaring, oftentimes not, as I made the decision to judge the operation anonymously.

It is far more expensive in both time and treasure to do it my way, but after years of traveling, of sometimes being forced to rely on guidebooks based merely on a rehash of some establishment's own inflated opinions, or even on questionnaires dispatched in lieu of personal observations, I have come to the conclusion that it is the only way.

RULES OF THE INN

Reservations, Deposits, and Rates Reservations are required for most of the inns and should be made as far in advance as possible, especially during peak travel times. Many inns require an advance deposit, an amount which may vary as much as the basic room rates. For obvious reasons specific rates are not quoted. Inexpensive means just that: less than an average motel room in the area. Expensive is equivalent to the tariff in a first-class hotel; very expensive equal to a super-luxe hotel. Moderate is somewhere in between.

Housekeeping In the smaller inns with shared baths the guest is responsible for cleaning the sink and tub. The rooms, often cleaned by the innkeeper doubling as chambermaid, should be kept in good order.

Tipping In the smaller places, discuss it with the innkeeper; many might be embarrassed by a gratuity or insulted by the offer but would welcome a thank-you note or the kind of bread-and-butter gift you would send if staying at someone's home.

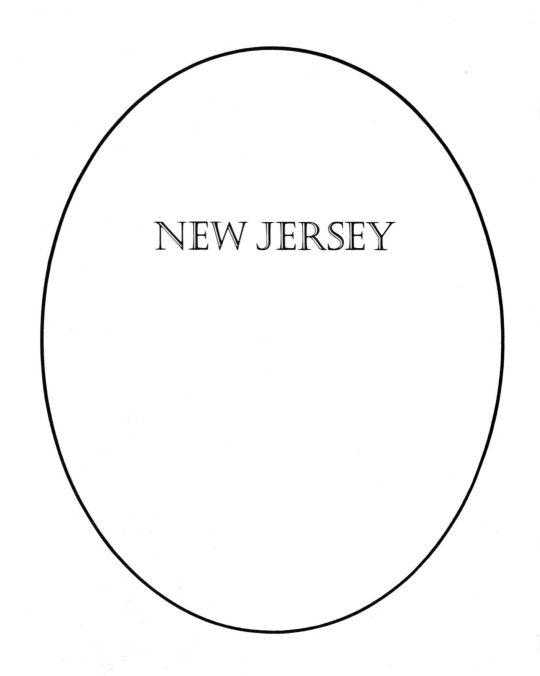

NEW JERSEY

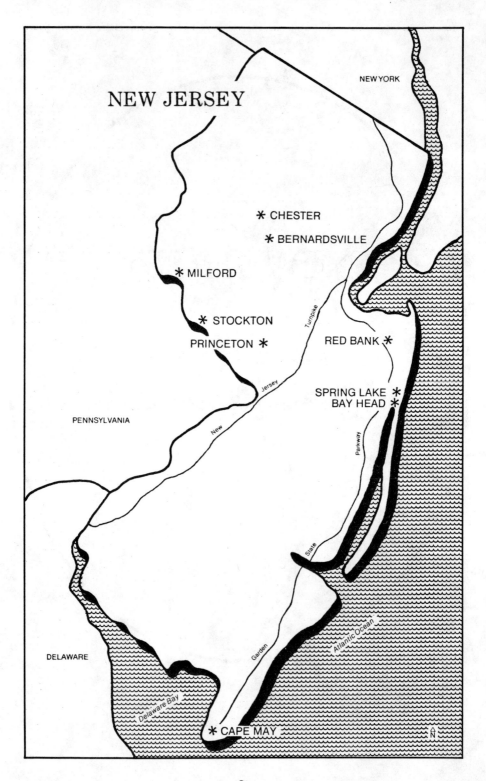

NEW JERSEY

NEW YORK

* CHESTER

* BERNARDSVILLE

* MILFORD

* STOCKTON

PRINCETON *

RED BANK *

SPRING LAKE *
BAY HEAD *

PENNSYLVANIA

Turnpike

Jersey

New

Parkway

State

Garden

Atlantic Ocean

DELAWARE

Delaware Bay

* CAPE MAY

N

2

CAPE MAY

Billed as "America's Oldest Seashore Resort," it is a National Historic Landmark town with close to six hundred reminders of the Golden Age of Tourism in the last half of the nineteenth century. And it has played host to southerners and northerners alike and to presidents since the days of Abraham Lincoln and Franklin Pierce. Honest Abe stayed at the Mansion House in 1849, a dozen years before his inauguration and 228 years after Dutch Captain Cornelius Jacobsen Mey first sailed into the bay, giving his name, which was later respelled, to the tip of the peninsula which pointed towards the sea. That was 1621, the year after the Pilgrims landed at Plymouth Rock, and Mey found the "climate charming and the land fruitful."

General Ulysses Grant relaxed in the salubrious seaside resort no fewer than four times and then came Chester Arthur. But it was Benjamin Harrison who, toward the end of the century, really established Cape May as a Summer White House—the first President to embark on what is now an accepted home away from home.

When Harrison was in residence there was an extensive beach front, which was similar enough to today's Daytona Beach to allow automobile races. A young Henry Ford in 1903 participated with one of his early inventions and apparently wanted to put his first automobile assembly plant in the area. But city fathers turned him down, concerned about keeping their idyllic seaside retreat the widest, longest and safest for bathing in the country—Florida then was an unknown peninsula, isolated and mosquito-ridden.

For a century, Cape May had been a watering hole for those who could take stagecoach, then rail and steamer, along the Delaware River and along the eastern shore. But the Great Fire of November 9, 1878, destroyed everything in a thirty-acre core of the city and tourism was halted. Only temporarily, however. Phoenix-like, the town rose from the ashes, and everywhere new and more solid structures rose from the sands, most of them built in the trendy Victorian style. And tourists today can arrive by a regularly scheduled ferry—a seventy-minute minicruise from Lewes, Delaware.

Today, Cape May is the exciting encapsulation of that grandly excessive, overly ornamented, gingerbread school of design, rivaled in its compact geography only by Eureka Springs in Arkansas. Cape May is a restful and spirit-soothing escape to a time when the pace was less hectic and the people were more accommodating and accessible, thriving in scenarios full of bustles and parasols, right out of a Victor Herbert operetta.

With a caring corps of city fathers and so many of the five thousand residents concerned about preserving the treasures of the past, Cape May today is a time capsule thrust backward into that past. In the heat of the summer season, when the population can explode tenfold, there may be a bit of a bustle and delays in the several excellent restaurants. But the wait is usually worthwhile; certainly it is at two of my favorite feederies, Alexanders' Inn at 653 Washington Street, set in a splendid Victorian home from 1883 (calves' liver Dubonnet with orange, country French rabbit, chicken chanterelle and sausage-nut strudel are memorable achievements) and at the Washington Inn close by, with a more predictable menu (try the veal Betsy, the lamb chops or the lump crabmeat sautéed in butter).

Also on Washington Street, at number 1048, is the Victorian Museum, housed in the delightfully curious 1881 Emlen Physick mansion designed by famed Philadelphia architect Frank Furness. Affiliated with the Mid-Atlantic Center for the Arts, the museum is headquarters for the dissemination of information on the special guided walking and trolley tours of the National Landmark District. On the grounds are also a Carriage House, home of the Cape May County Art League, and another building containing an interesting exhibit of antique tools.

On Ocean Street at the town's Washington Street Mall is an information booth, easy to find on the pedestrian walkways opened in 1971. The mall, in the original downtown shopping district, is an intelligent answer to commercial encroachment. Park benches, trees, bushes, flowers are everywhere, along with a variety of shopping and eating experiences that do not shout.

At Christmas time, the Washington Street Mall is center stage for old-fashioned fun: candlelight walks, store windows, gaslights wreathed in green and red and carolers strolling and bands playing. At Christmas time, several of the inns of Cape May do special things: decorating trees and parlours in authentic Victorian style, stringing popcorn and other foodstuffs, using candles everywhere and taking wonderful old toys out of storage.

But at any time of the year these inns are special. There are many of them, appealing to all tastes and pocketbooks, although I do have favorites. Here is the current list of Tolf's Top Ten—

The Abbey

THE ABBEY
Cape May, New Jersey

Despite its ambitious sixty-foot tower which lacks only a spire and cross, its ruby glass windows arched in the Gothic grand manner and an irresistible air of dedication, this abbey was never a house of worship. It was named The Abbey when the Schatz team, Jay and Marianne, took over. It is an apt name, not only for its Victorian Gothic resemblance to a church, but for the religious fervour with which the Schatzes approach their never-ending tasks of restoring this treasure to its full glory.

Built in the years of the Reconstruction by a wealthy U.S. senator, John B. McCreary, The Abbey is clearly one of the great landmarks in a city of landmarks. Much the same could be said about its owners, refugees from the corporate world, in this case the chemical and steel industries. Lovers of the old and rare, they are meticulous restorers, proud of every curlicue of gingerbread trim, every brush stroke of paint, every period antique found somewhere and placed in exactly the right spot.

What have they been doing in recent months? Recently they replaced wall and archway between parlor and library, gracing this room with a pair of out-size antique bookcases. But there is still more wallpapering to do, this time in the Saratoga Room where the ceiling was being revitalized and plans made for removing the closet added in the 1920s and returning to the roots with a Victorian armoire.

The Schatz hunters also found a tester bed for their New Orleans room and still more hats for a collection that is approaching the preposterous. It is all in fun—and that too is part of the Schatz approach to innkeeping. They are obviously enjoying keeping alive their acquired trust, in finding all the right furnishings and in sharing their love of antiques and their respect for the Cape May past.

And the Schatzes certainly have fun with their guests. Explaining the origins of the possessions, the harp in the back parlor, the vintage lamps and plantstands, the converted gaslight chandeliers or the window treatments that look Moorish in design and concept. There are other special cornice draperies in the recently restored dining room with its wonderful tables and elaborately carved chests. This dining room is where Abbey guests are served breakfasts during spring and fall months, while in the summer, the morning awakeners are served on the veranda. Afternoon refreshments are taken in parlor, veranda, wherever, but that is after the departure of the last tourists, those who have not been fortunate enough to overnight upstairs. At five o'clock sharp, Thursday through Sunday there are guided tours of the treasure trove on the first floor.

THE ABBEY, Columbia Avenue and Gurney Street, Cape May, New Jersey 08204. Telephone: (609) 884-4506. Accommodations: seven rooms; four private baths; no telephones; no televisions. Rates: moderate to expensive, includes breakfast. No children under 12. No pets. Cards: MC, VISA. Open April–November.

Getting There: The Abbey is impossible to miss; it is on the corner of two of the main streets in the small town.

Breakfast with a Capital B
BARNARD-GOOD HOUSE
Cape May, New Jersey

"Love continues to be our theme as it has since we began. . . . Our love for wonderful and unique Cape May. . . ." Thus begins the cool blue brochure assembled by innkeepers Nan and Tom Hawkins, who have embossed their message with a wonderful border of sea and shore climaxed by a pair of mermaids sitting happily in their shells. The unique colors, the laciness, the eye-appealing artwork are typical of the Hawkins' approach to innkeeping.

Thus, when they painted their dormered mansard-crowned three-story what they prefer to think of as West Coast Victorian—blue, raspberry and tan—others of lesser faith (knowledge or imagination) went into a state of Cape May shock, dismissing the Second Empire Victorian as "that purple house." The purists might also dismiss the "Hawkins' Turkish Corner" because it has an Indian elephant pedestal table and a Chinese Buddha in it. But what could be more Victorian, what could be more truly representative of the eclectic nature of that over-exuberant period of American design?

Their pride and joy is named for their great-grandparents. Each of the rooms bears the name of one or another relative and the Hawkins have added to the tribute by filling the rooms with a fine collection of

Barnard Good House

period antiques. I especially like the pump organ and the false fireplace in the living room, put there for show a century ago.

The dining room draws similar raves, not only for the converted brass-pewter gas chandelier and the giant sideboard, but for what has to be the best breakfast this side of Schenectady. Nan brews, bakes, squeezes and cooks up a Cape May storm with all kinds of impossible-to-resist delights. If croissants, casseroles and crêpes are the food of love , play on Nan, play on.

BARNARD-GOOD HOUSE, 238 Perry Street, Cape May, New Jersey 08204. Telephone: (609) 884-5381. Accommodations: five rooms; one private bath; one suite with private bath; no telephones; no televisions. Rates: moderate, includes breakfast. No children under 12. No pets. Cards: MC, VISA. Open April 1 through November 5.

Getting There: From Beach Avenue drive west on Perry Street or Jackson Street to the intersection of the two; the inn is on the corner.

There's Class in Brass
BRASS BED INN
Cape May, New Jersey

A survivor of the Great Fire of 1878, this close-to-the-beach (two blocks) cottage is a Gothic Revival gem that was originally built as two separate structures, one of them housing the servants and the heat of the kitchen. In 1930 they were joined together and the union was called the Woodbine Tourist Home. That decade was not the high point of Cape May prosperity or popularity, however. Nor were the 1940s or the 1950s, nor the 1960s or 1970s. This wooden frame echo of the Gilded Age was not reborn until 1980. That is when John and Donna Dunwoody arrived on the scene, took charge of the memory bank and worked the marvels of a masterly executed restoration.

In the process they scraped off old layers of paint, searched for the original colors, found some of the original furnishings which were brought into the home in 1872, and found a brass bed for each and every room. Vintage of course. They also replaced the wallpaper, located pictures appropriate for the period, a matched five-piece Renaissance Revival parlor suite and a walnut bookcase that is a tribute to some forgotten cabinetmaker. It now houses a fine collection

9

of reference material pertaining to the Victorian Era and the nistory of Cape May.

Also recently added as part of the never-ending improvements dedicated innkeepers constantly strive for (and achieve when they can afford it) is the year-round solarium adjacent to the dining room (with the portraits of John's great-grandparents). It is a happy retreat on cold days when one still seeks the sun. In the summer, there is the beach (hot and cold outside showers are alongside the inn for washing off the sand), and the wonderful porch, freshly painted and lined with wicker and rockers.

At Christmas time, the Dunwoody clan celebrates a Victorian holiday, trimming their tree with glass ornaments that have been in the family a half century, stringing their own popcorn strands, setting up the old Lionel train and bringing out the dollhouse.

BRASS BED INN, 719 Columbia Avenue, Cape May, New Jersey 08204. Telephone: (609) 884-8075. Accommodations: eight rooms; private baths; no telephones; no televisions. Rates: inexpensive to moderate, includes breakfast. No children under 12. No pets. Cards: MC, VISA. Open all year.

Getting There: Columbia Avenue, three blocks from Ocean Street, is the main inns thoroughfare; the Brass Bed is in the midst of the complex.

Cap Would Be Proud of This One
CAPTAIN MEY'S INN
Cape May, New Jersey

This fine three-story Victorian was constructed in 1890 by a local doctor who practiced homeopathic medicine, Walter H. Phillips, not by the Dutch captain who first explored this point of Jersey peninsula in 1620. But it does honor the name. In many ways.

The last weekend in April the inn and town sponsor an annual tulip festival. More than twenty-five thousand bulbs from Holland are planted throughout the city; there are all kinds of Dutch cookies and treats in stores, inns and homes; there is a typically Dutch *straatwassen,* a scrubbing of the streets; and dancing in wooden shoes called *klompen.* At Christmas the inn trims three different trees in the Dutch

Captain Mey's Inn

manner, and the traditions of that predecessor of Santa Claus known as Saint Nicholas are honored. High on the rooftop is ol' Saint Nick, clothed in red velvet, crowned with a mitre hat and riding a white horse accompanied by Black Piet.

Innkeepers Milly LaCanfora and Carin Feddermann are proud of the inn's heritage. They are happy to keep alive the memory of the founder, the explorer, who became governor of the New Netherlands in 1623 and who was instructed by his monarch to "govern by love and friendship rather than by force."

In the inn's guest rooms are various Dutch artifacts; in the recently restored dining room is a beautifully carved oak mantel framing imported Delft tile. They even serve Dutch cheeses as part of the full breakfast, which is served on the veranda in summer and in the candlelit dining room, accompanied by classical music in the winter.

A recent restoration at Captain Mey's is the staircase, completed just in time for the beginning of another season. It took three months to scrape away all the old white paint, revealing the rich oak which now flanks the burgundy runner held in place with polished brass rods. On the walls, shrimp-colored Shumucker wallpaper was put up.

By the time you visit, the tireless ladies, seeking to improve and perfect their tribute to Captain May, will no doubt be engaged in some other project, finding still more memorabilia to fill their century-old living monument.

CAPTAIN MEY'S INN, 202 Ocean Street, Cape May, New Jersey 08204. Telephone: (609) 884-7793. Accommodations: eight rooms; two private baths; no telephones; no televisions. Rates: moderate, includes full breakfast and afternoon tea and refreshments. No children under 12. No pets. Cards: MC, VISA. Open all year.

Getting There: The inn is two blocks from the beach and one-half-block from the Washington Street Mall, across from the public library.

THE CHALFONTE
Cape May, New Jersey

Would you believe spoonbread, beaten-out-back biscuits, Virginia country ham, kidney stew, Southern fried chicken in Cape May? The Carolinas of course, but on the southern shore of New Jersey? Check into this 1876 galleried, white Victorian steamboat gothic ghost of Cape May's distant past and you'll become a believer. And probably a convert to the kind of seaside and mountain resort hotels that used to dominate the landscapes of many vacation spots in this country. The Chalfonte, purchased in 1983 by the team which had managed it for the previous decade, Anne LeDuc and Judy Bartella, is a special experience.

Victorian, yes. Antique-filled, charming, no. But certainly an experience, especially for someone whose mouth is watering for some down-home honest Southern cookin' with lots of soul. Helen Dickerson is responsible for that. Back in the 1940s she was brought on board by the owner, Mrs. Calvin Satterfield, who took over the giant in 1915 and has been there ever since. In recent years she has also been on local television shows and featured in numerous publications, along with her daughter and assistant, Dot, for feeding all those hungry faces which come back year after year.

And they have no doubt noticed considerable improvement over the last few years. Sparked by $20,000 in federal funds matching private contributions and aided greatly by the innovative Chalfonte Work Weekends, during which volunteers work six hours a day

repairing and restoring in exchange for room and board, the Grande Dame is beginning to recover some of that old luster and shine.

THE CHALFONTE, 301 Howard Street, Cape May, New Jersey 08204. Telephone: (609) 884-8409. Accommodations: 72 rooms; some private baths; no telephones; no televisions. Rates: inexpensive to moderate. Full bar and meal service. Children permitted. No pets. Cards: MC, VISA. Open Memorial Day Weekend and from mid-June to Labor Day and weekends through the middle of October.

Getting There: From Beach Drive take Howard three blocks to Sewell and the impossible-to-miss hotel.

Forget the Dutch
THE DUKE OF WINDSOR INN
Cape May, New Jersey

This just might be the only establishment in the American hospitality industry to recognize the folly, the love and devotion of what one ruling monarch gave up for "the woman I love." Why is it here in Cape May, a Victorian memory bank with all kinds of remembrances of the Dutch? Because twice-divorced Wallis Warfield Simpson of Baltimore made her debut in Cape May. She might have made several others, but it was here that innkeepers Bruce and Fran Prichard chose to memorialize, using the name for an 1896 mansion happily converted to inn. It's part of the Queen Anne eclecticism of the Victorian Age, and a handsome one at that, with Tiffany windows, finely molded ceiling medallions, period furnishings, including original brass beds and lamps and a dominating tower of close to fifty feet.

The top of the tower rooms are reached by a vaulting, sweeping three-story staircase, followed by paneled wainscotting. There are a couple of corner fireplaces set into the common rooms where guests relax with afternoon tea or with a complimentary Continental breakfast. These are enjoyed under a ceiling latticed with curved moldings and surrounded by walls wainscotted with the deeply embossed covering known as Lincrusta and accented by galley railings holding a platter collection. There is a commodious grandeur in the inn; the guest rooms are more spacious than most, the ceilings are blessedly high and there often seems to be more windows than walls.

14

THE DUKE OF WINDSOR INN, 817 Washington Street, Cape May, New Jersey 08204. Telephone: (609) 884-1355. Accommodations: nine rooms; four private baths; no telephones; no televisions. Rates: inexpensive to moderate, includes Continental breakfast and afternoon tea. Children under 12 not permitted. No pets. Cards: MC, VISA. Open every day from June 15–November 1, weekends after that.

Getting There: Washington Street runs from the mall of the same name directly to the inn.

The Name Says It All

THE GINGERBREAD HOUSE
Cape May, New Jersey

Block-long Gurney Street runs from inn-filled Columbia Avenue to the beach, and is where the row of Stockton summer cottages were built in 1869 as part of the massive Stockton Hotel, one of Cape May's giants in the good old days. One of these cottages was built with fireplace, and that is the one Fred and Joan Echevarria bought and began to restore in 1980.

One of the smaller inns in my top ten, the Gingerbread House is perfectly named, so laden is its exterior with the kind of trim that carpenters and woodworkers turned out by the mile at the turn of the century. The gaily striped awning out front provides a colorful contrast to the pristine white and green trim of this three-story, sandwiched between its neighbors.

Rooms are not large, but they are immaculate and tastefully furnished with wicker and a few period artifacts here and there. The Gingerbread House is not an antique-crammed minimuseum; it is far homier in atmosphere and setting. And that is the appeal, aided mightily by the casual warmth of the innkeepers. They are new to what can often be a frustrating occupation, but they are certainly good at what they do.

THE GINGERBREAD HOUSE, 28 Gurney Street, Cape May, New Jersey 08204. Telephone: (609) 884-0211. Accommodations: six rooms; three private baths; no telephones; no televisions. Rates: inexpensive to moderate, includes Continental breakfast. Children under five not permitted. No pets. No cards. Open all year.

Getting There: Gurney Street is between Stockton Place and Ocean Street and is reached by Beach Drive or Columbia Avenue.

A Stay Here Is No Gamble

MAINSTAY INN & THE COTTAGE
Cape May, New Jersey

In the heart of old Cape May, on a road replete with inn after privately owned home after inn, the Mainstay Inn is undoubtedly the most photographed, the most talked-about reincarnation in a town where residents and visitors alike spend hours and days and weeks talking about their city's rebirth.

Built in 1872 by a pair of wealthy gamblers who wanted a private, elegant oasis to pursue their pleasures, the Mainstay Inn is an intensely Italianate villa with uniquely over-long pillars gracefully framing the broadsweep of a veranda. It is as stunning today as it must have been to the tourists of Cape May in its heyday. Ground floor ceilings are fourteen feet high; there is a plethora of richly formed plaster medallions and moldings; and a wonderfully wide center hall staircase, as much an eye-catcher inside as that fence and the well-kept gardens on the outside. Exquisitely chosen furnishings complement glistening cut-glass brass gasoliers, luxuriant lace curtains and tucked-in draperies, heavily carved headboards and chests, giant mirrors and the kind of accent pieces treasured by Victorians.

Since the early 1970s the Mainstay Inn, formerly the Victorian Mansion (which housed a minimuseum) but born as the Jackson Clubhouse, has been in the tender loving hands of the Carrolls, Tom and Sue. Indeed, they are the mainstay of the Mainstay, a happy couple devoted to the proposition that the past must be preserved and made available to those in the present in as perfect a state as possible. To that end, they not only take in overnight guests but also give afternoon tours of the inn. Afternoon tea is offered to tour-takers as well as to those fortunate enough to be spending the night. The vintage Victorian guest rooms are named for the presidents who have vacationed in Cape May as well as for other distinguished Americans.

There are five other similarly furnished bedrooms in the neighboring 1870 house, a fourteen-room home the Carrolls recently restored. Known as The Cottage, the new Carroll acquisition offers modern private baths with all the amenities. It is joined to the Mainstay by a walkway that, of course, is framed by flowers and embraced by that extraordinary fence, which in its own way forms the perfect wraparound for this eye-pleasing gem.

MAINSTAY INN and THE COTTAGE, 635 Columbia Avenue, Cape May, New Jersey 08204. Telephone: (609) 884-8690. Accommodations: 13 rooms; nine private baths; no telephones; no televisions. Rates: moderate to expensive, includes breakfast and afternoon tea. "Young children generally find us tiresome; heavy smokers find us intolerant." No pets. No cards. Open April 1 to November 30.

Getting There: Columbia Avenue is the main "inn avenue" in town; from Beach Drive it is two blocks taking Gurney, Stockton or Howard Streets.

Mainstay Inn. Cape May.   Eloth Hewitt

17

God Save the Queen
THE QUEEN VICTORIA
Cape May, New Jersey

The year 1981 was the happiest of birthday celebrations in Cape May. It was the centennial of the Douglas Gregory House, reopened in all its Victorian glory as an inn by Joan and Dane Wells, innkeepers extraordinaire. Dane is a master craftsman and catalyst to many a community's realization of their obligations to the present and future as trustees of the past. Joan was one-time Director of the Victorian Society in America and Curator of the Molly Brown House Museum in Denver. Under her leadership some $400,000 was pumped into the revitalization of that mansion. Together the Wells team tried to purchase a property in northern California to convert an abandoned hospital to country inn, but the necessary approvals could not be obtained and they looked elsewhere.

California's loss is most certainly Cape May's gain. The Wells' expertise is reflected in *Crown & Thistle,* their own publication. *Crown & Thistle* reports the local calendar of activities, from springtime tulip festivals to Christmas celebrations, and on their own endless pursuits and improvements (most recently, the replacement of the mansard roof, adding a pair of bedrooms, and upgrading the gardens) and adds a recipe or two. The most requested one is the Queen's Oats, a granola-type assemblage described as "a very flexible recipe, and rarely comes out the same way twice for us." It's best served with honey that comes from Joan's brother's own beehives in Montana.

The Queen's Oats are frequently on the breakfast buffet table along with freshly baked bread, some kind of farm-fresh eggs, freshly squeezed juice and excellent coffee and teas. There is more tea in the afternoon, and that too is spread out on the dining room buffet table— Victorian of course—with an assortment of more goodies.

The front parlour, set in one of the corner tower bays, has the Wells' collection of mission furniture. Some pieces are from that campus of craftsmen in East Aurora, New York known as Roycroft (which is now a country inn described in my *Country Inns of New York State.*) There are other pieces which carry out the Victorian theme with great panache. Alistair Cooke could film a segment of *Masterpiece Theater* in this inn with its guestrooms named after such illustrious figures as Charles Dickens, Lily Langtry and the Prince of Wales.

The Queen Victoria

There is additional honoring of Victorian immortals at Christmastime. That's when there are readings from Dickens, street caroling, special meals and special decorations. The Queen Victoria has not one, but three Christmas trees, each reflecting a different period of the long, sixty-four-year reign of the beloved monarch. One is laden chiefly with various edibles, another from the mid-Victorian period with toys and small gifts and a third has some manufactured ornaments along with vintage greeting cards.

In every way the Wells devote themselves to their chosen tasks of recreating something special with great style and verve. Any married couple that can hang more than two hundred rolls of wallpaper and still remain on speaking terms has my unqualified respect!

THE QUEEN VICTORIA, 102 Ocean Street, Cape May, New Jersey 08204. Telephone: (609) 884-8702. Accommodations: 12 rooms; eight private baths; no telephones; no televisions. Rates: moderate to expensive, includes breakfast, afternoon tea, use of bicycles. Inquire about children. No pets. Cards: MC, VISA. Smoking not permitted in guest rooms. Open all year.

Getting There: On the main road entering Cape May, Lafayette Street, turn left past Jefferson and Franklin at Ocean Street, the second traffic light; the inn is three blocks down on the right.

Roses, Roses Everywhere

VICTORIAN ROSE
Cape May, New Jersey

The same year Joan and Dane Wells celebrated a centennial by opening their Queen Victoria, another couple, Bob and Linda Mullock, opened their pride and joy: a sherbet-colored two-story cottage designed by the same Stephen Decatur Button responsible for the Jackson Clubhouse (now the Mainstay Inn) a couple of Victorian memory banks down the road. Both were built in 1872, this one as a summer home for a prosperous Philadelphian. In later years, it was a school for girls (interestingly enough, Linda is a former Montessori teacher), then a tea room and finally the Southern Inn, open to overnight guests.

In converting their avocation into occupation, the Mullocks were true to the name: the rose garden out front and alongside is absolutely fantastic. But then so too are the chrysanthemums and the many flowers they force into bloom for celebration of the Christmas season. Their tree is trimmed with—what else—roses, and their living room fireplace crackles with good cheer as guests rally around after candlelight touring or caroling.

In the mornings the Cape May pilgrims gather around the massive carved oak table, ringed with high-back chairs and graced with the Mullock's assortment of antique dishes and serving pieces. The Continental breakfast is laid out on the overwhelming mirrored sideboard which was once in the Boardman home—Boardman designed Atlantic City's famed boardwalk.

Another prized possession with a history is the Victorian bed in the ground floor room: it used to be part of the museum collection in the Emlen Physick mansion.

VICTORIAN ROSE, 715 Columbia Avenue, Cape May, New Jersey 08204. Telephone: (609) 884-2497. Accommodations: ten rooms; eight private baths; no telephones; no television; two apartments with private bath and kitchen for weekly rental; a cottage, the "Innlett," sleeps five and has private bath and kitchen. Rates: moderate, includes Continental breakfast. Inquire about children and pets. No cards. Closed from December to April.

Getting There: The inn is on the same street as the Chalfonte and the Mainstay Inn, next door to the Brass Bed Inn.

Conover's Country Charm
CONOVER'S BAY HEAD INN
Bay Head, New Jersey

Innkeepers Carl and Beverly Conover should certainly have their name in the title of their happy domain: they work constantly to ensure the comfort of their guests, and in the off-season, when they shut down for a few weeks, they take paintbrushes in hand and start redecorating. And when they find time at other seasons of the year, they are off antique-hunting, searching the byways of Jersey for special chests, wiggly wood tables, hand-carved headboards. Each of their rooms boasts something special: one is filled with various steam gauges (steam engines hold a particular fascination for Carl) and another has an out-size Victorian bed. And most recently, the Conovers have finished restoring a pair of iron-brass beds and will be putting them into their inn about the time this book hits bookstore shelves.

Beverly has color-coordinated the drapes, spreads, wallpaper, pillows and doilies, which she has sewn and crocheted. And every day she bakes something special for serving in the dining room or for guests to carry out to some shady spot on the lawn. In the off-season the breakfasts become more bountiful, and there are always flowers and plants to refresh the eye and a multitude of books to furnish the mind. Porch rocking chairs are popular in the summer as is the fireplace in the winter. In colder months, when the Atlantic no longer beckons, the Conovers direct their guests to the hundred antique shops that are within a couple miles radius. And for the more athletic-minded, there is Twilight Lake for ice skating.

The Conovers' pride and joy is the perfect inn for the quiet little community of Bay Head, one without neon, billboards or even fast-food feeders. It is hard to believe that it is only sixty miles from New York and sixty-five from Philadelphia.

CONOVER'S BAY HEAD INN, 646 Main Avenue, Bay Head, New Jersey 08742. Telephone: (201) 892-4664. Accommodations: 12 rooms; two with private baths; no telephones; no televisions. Rates: inexpensive to moderate, includes complimentary breakfast and wine. Inquire about children. No pets. Cards: MC, VISA. Open February–December.

Getting There: Bay Head is south of Point Pleasant Beach and north of Manasquan on State Route 35 South. The inn is one and a half blocks south of the town's third traffic light.

Seaside Victorian Comfort

ASHLING COTTAGE
Spring Lake, New Jersey

Located on the Jersey shore between Red Bank in the north and Bay Head to the south, the seaside settlement of Spring Lake was known at the turn of the century as the Newport of New Jersey. Cottages large and small were built along shady streets and lanes which circle its three lakes: its small namesake in the center and two at each flank, Lake Como and Wreck Pond. A mile and a half long boardwalk was constructed and bathhouses were erected at each end in beach pavilions which feature a pair of excellent saltwater pools.

Between the ocean and the spring-fed, crystal clear lake with its winding rock garden paths and rows of weeping willows, is the Ashling Cottage, built in 1877 by Spring Lake resident George Hulett. Additions in later years made the solidly built three-story Victorian rambler more spacious while retaining the distinctive touches of the original builder. Hulett luxuriated in an almost show-off kind of diversity, making no two rooms alike, installing dormer windows and tucking first- and second-floor porches here and there on the structure.

The result is pure Victorian and innkeepers goodi and Jack Stewart (yes, with a small g), who celebrated their March 1984 purchase with a St. Patrick's Day party on the premises, have taken care to preserve the spirit with their furnishings. They also have dedicated themselves to the proposition that as first-time innkeepers they are going to go the extra step—sometimes in this most trying of all trades it turns out to be a mile—to ensure their guests' comforts. This translates to individual wake-up calls, complimentary breakfasts—early or late and served in a warm, wicker-filled side porch all pink and inviting or brought on bed trays for special occasions. Adding to individual guests' one-time celebrations will be those planned and executed by the Stewarts to mark some holiday or event.

They will also make dinner reservations in their special town. The Sandpiper two blocks away is as conveniently located as it is easy to

23

Ashling Cottage

recommend. Included on their menu are snapper Duglere and walnut torte—although it is a bring-your-own wine place.

Ashling Cottage is as immaculately maintained as everything else seems to be in this oasis of a seaside spread. The Spring Lake Park across the street sometimes looks as if it is swept every hour. A fine view of this park with its sparkling water can be seen from room number 1 of the inn. There are three windows and an array of unique furnishings: a hat rack with a spring garden collection, art deco glass shades, a step-up bathroom and a special oak bureau with mirror.

ASHLING COTTAGE, 106 Sussex Avenue, Spring Lake, New Jersey 07762. Telephone: (201) 449-3553. Accommodations: 10 rooms; eight private baths; no telephones; television in common room. Rates: moderate to expensive. Children permitted. No pets. Cards: AE, MC, VISA. Open March—December.

Getting There: Take Exit 98 from the Garden State Parkway, following State Road 34 and Spring Lake signs 1.5 miles to the traffic circle; from there take Allaire Road one block to Warren Avenue around the lake to First Avenue; a left turn leads to Sussex Avenue and the inn.

Waterfront Colonial
MOLLY PITCHER INN
Red Bank, New Jersey

If you wonder who Molly Pitcher was—or is—just read the place mat in the spacious dining room of this Georgian Colonial brick building which looks as though it was removed from the campus of some Ivy League college. It explains that she was the wife of one John Casper Hays, a barber from Carlisle, Pennsylvania, who served in the Seventh Regiment, and that she not only survived the harshness of the Valley Forge winter, but that she also somehow found herself in the midst of the battle at Freehold on a Sunday morning in June 1778. When a British bullet took her husband out of action, she picked up the musket and, according to a dispatch of the time, "like a Spartan heroine fought with astonishing bravery discharging the piece with as much regularity as any soldier present."

Poised majestically on the banks of the Navesink River, the inn named for the indomitable Molly has expanded over the years and is now flanked by a motel, a large swimming pool and has a terraced patio which overlooks the blue waters leading off to the gentle greens of faraway hills and low-lying mountains and the inn's marina—if you arrive by boat arrange in advance for dockage.

The walls of windows in the dining rooms look out at this idyllic scene, so close to the New York-Newark megalopolis. In wintertime there is a fleet of ice boats to watch; in warmer months the many private yachts which dock at the inn for an overnight or for one of their easy-to-recommend meals.

Breakfast is buffet, if desired, and luncheon features a variety of fresh salads and all kinds of sandwiches and burgers. The evening menu is changed daily and reflects the vagaries of local market supply. When I last stayed at the Molly Pitcher they had fresh swordfish and tile fish along with pan-fried trout almondine, beer-batter shrimp with a rather sweet orange sauce, prime rib and smoked loin of pork served, of course, with sauerkraut.

For dinner you might also visit the nearby Olde Union House, which also overlooks the Navesink. Their crab-stuffed mushroom caps, soft shells and veal entrées are excellent, their wine list smart enough to have Amarone and there is live entertainment and dancing on the weekends.

Rooms at the Molly Pitcher are motel-modern and carefully maintained. They provide a comfortable retreat after a day exploring the peninsula, which is triangled by the Navesink and Shrewsbury Rivers wending their way to the Atlantic. Close by is Fort Monmouth with its Signal Corps Museum, the Garden State Arts Center and Monmouth Park Race Track. Golfers and beachgoers head for the Bamm Hollow Country Club and deep-sea fishermen for the Oceanic Marina in Rumson. In Freehold, site of Molly's heroics, there is the National Broadcasters Hall of Fame and the Monmouth County Historical Museum and Library.

MOLLY PITCHER INN, State Highway 35, 88 Riverside Avenue, Red Bank, New Jersey 07701. Telephone: (201) 747-2500. Accommodations: 110 rooms; private baths; telephones; televisions. Rates: moderate. Full bar and meal service. Children permitted. No pets. Cards: AE, MC, VISA. Open all year.

Getting There: Take exit 11 of New Jersey Turnpike and proceed south on State Road 35 to Red Bank; the inn is in the center of town and is clearly marked.

A Nugget of Nostalgia

PUBLICK HOUSE

Chester, New Jersey

The full name is Black River & Raritan Publick House. And since the celebration of this country's bicentennial it has been part of the expanding portfolio of Growth Enterprises, which takes credit for several other nuggets of nostalgia in New Jersey: Whitehouse Junction in Whitehouse and The Store in Basking Ridge, along with The Office in Cranford, Morristown and Summit. This historic old tavern was established in 1810 by one Zephaniah Drake, whose local line of stagecoaches made it a regular stop on the run between New York City and Easton, Pennsylvania. Growth Enterprises spent no little time and treasure restoring, reconstructing and reviving the spirit and the traditions of the time of Drake and subsequent innkeepers.

The result today is sheer fun. In each of the four dining rooms, as well as in the Barbershop Lounge, which has more to do with singing quartets than with cutting hair, is a fascinating array of artifacts to keep the eyes busy while trying to concentrate on the food. When I last

lunched here, I ate in the room with the kind of ice chest I think I can vaguely remember as a very young boy in the heartlands; I certainly remember those cast iron skillets and those fry pans my grandmother always called spiders.

Not even the restrooms escape the backward-looking decorator: the mens' room is filled with old advertisements and business records. But none of the distractions affect the food. My cheddar cheese soup, my monkfish, that poor man's lobster, the chicken and cheese sticks crisply fried and just begging to be dipped in a fine honey-mustard sauce, were all excellent. And I liked the happy attitudes of the staff.

The building is on the National Register of Historic Places and its present owners have kept alive the spirit of the stagecoach past in their second- and third-story rooms. There is nothing ultra-elegant, nothing overblown here, but then neither was there in the early years of the nineteenth century for passengers bouncing along roads which alternated between a parade of muddy potholes and shake-em-up corduroy log affairs. The rooms have a simple charm, a sense of belonging to a different time, and there is a carefully selected sprinkling of antiques, of special prints and photographs on the walls.

PUBLICK HOUSE, 111 Main Street, Chester, New Jersey 07930. Telephone: (201) 879-4800. Accommodations: 10 rooms and suites; private baths; telephones; no televisions. Rates: moderate, includes Continental breakfast. Full bar and meal service including Sunday brunch. Children permitted. No pets. Cards: AE, MC, VISA. Open all year.

Getting There: The inn is impossible to miss: it is on the main street of the town, State Road 24.

Hay Loft Happening

OLD MILL INN

Bernardsville, New Jersey

In the so-called Skylands region of New Jersey, south of Chester and the state's largest lake, Hopatcong, is this old mill memory of the Revolutionary War. Built in 1768 to store grain for a grist mill across the road, and eleven years later used to warehouse supplies for Washington's army encamped in the area, the inn is really a barn, handsomely converted to a popular restaurant and lodgings. Patrons elbow into a bar that was built in the old stable and eat in dining rooms that for years were used to store grain and wagons which carted the product from grower to mill to consumer.

Overnight guests are accommodated in small and simply furnished rooms located in the old hay lofts. Washington's army no doubt would have found them luxurious, but today's traveler might prefer the hundred-room motel which is across the spacious parking lot. Popular with the several major corporations in the Bernardsville area as a conference center and as temporary housing, it is still a motel.

For the history, the back-to-the-farm feeling, I prefer the Old Mill Inn with its sense of the past and its recognition of the present in its restaurant. Their menu is solid, filled with beef, chops, mixed grill and all-American Continental adjustments such as veal cordon bleu and Oscar, Long Island duckling in a bing cherry sauce, shrimp scampi. They do have roast pheasant stuffed with a mélange of apples, onions and chopped parsley then doused with an apple jack cream sauce and they do serve a special bouillabaisse, and for dessert, plum pudding.

OLD MILL INN, U.S. Highway 202, Bernardsville, New Jersey 07924. Telephone: (201) 221-1100. Accommodations: seven rooms; private baths; telephones; no television. Rates: inexpensive. Children permitted. No pets. Cards: AE, MC, VISA. Open all year.

Getting There: The inn is on the corner of U.S. Highway 202 and North Maple Avenue West.

Colonial College Inn with Class
THE NASSAU INN
Princeton, New Jersey

What the Hanover Inn is to Dartmouth and the Carolina Inn to Chapel Hill, The Nassau Inn is to Princeton. Located across the street from that pleasant, ivy-covered campus, the inn's name has the same inspiration as the town's Nassau Street and the University's Nassau Hall: King William III of the House of Nassau.

The inn hasn't been here as long as the university, which moved to the town of Princeton—or Prince's Town—a quarter century earlier. But it does date back to 1756 and its entrance has more than an architectural patina of age, and its lobby with its massive fireplace and heavily beamed ceilings, its rich paneling and sense of spaciousness, exudes Colonial charm. The trio of restaurants, especially the Tap Room with its own cheery hearth and its dark woods, march right along to the Colonial fife and drum.

But once past the entrance and into the rooms, the feeling is more modern. This is one historic inn that does not believe in sacrificing the amenities to tradition. Not only are the rooms as comfortable and up-to-date as any hotel or motel of class, but there is also a swimming pool, an outdoor cafe, ample convention and meeting facilities and all kinds of banqueting possibilities. It is the perfect base camp for parents visiting their progeny smart enough to get into Princeton, or for alumni wondering how they ever were admitted, or simply for tourists who want to stroll through one of the loveliest college campuses in the nation and then explore the area's other historic wonders.

West on Mercer Street is the Princeton Battlefield State Park commemorating Washington's all-important, morale-boosting victory over the British on January 3, 1777. Close by, at the corner of Witherspoon and Wiggins Streets, is the Princeton Cemetery, with graves of many who fell in the struggle and in other battles in this state, known as the "Pathway of the Revolution" (close to a hundred battles were fought in the colony which is 166 miles long and only 32 wide). Jersey-born Grover Cleveland is buried here, as is Paul Tulane, founder of Tulane University in New Orleans, and both of the Burrs, Aaron Sr. and Jr.

The Bainbridge House at 158 Nassau Street was the birthplace of William Bainbridge, commander of *Old Ironsides*. It is now headquarters for the Princeton Historical Society, which has a small museum in the 1766 building. At 15 Hodge Road is the 1854 home occupied by Grover Cleveland after serving as President. The Friends Meeting House by Quaker Road was used as a hospital after the Battle of Princeton, and the 1758 structure is still open for religious services. The Morven home at 55 Stockton Street, built in the 1750s and, for a time, the governor's mansion, has had a succession of distinguished residents: Richard Stockton, a signer of the Declaration of Independence, and General Cornwallis, along with the governors of the state, who now have their official residence elsewhere.

NASSAU INN, Palmer Square (P.O. Box 668), Princeton, New Jersey 08540. Telephone: (609) 921-7500. Accommodations: 221 rooms; private baths; telephones; color television; AM/FM radios. Rates: expensive. Children permitted. No pets. Cards: AE, MC, VISA. Open all year.

Getting There: Palmer Square is in the center of town, directly across the street from the university.

Bucolic Retreat
THE WOOLVERTON INN
Stockton, New Jersey

One of the better—if not the best—New Jersey answers to the ancient and honorable Pennsylvania innkeeping across the Delaware River is this 1793 three-story stone bulwark north of New Hope. Surrounded by ten acres of country replete with sheep, dairy cows and deer, the Woolverton is contained by a classic white fence and shaded by giant trees that might have been planted by the same John Prall who quarried the stone for his home out back. Prall also ran the local gristmill, located where the Delaware meets the Wichecheoke Creek.

The house that John built was remodeled a century later by a Woolverton who was pretentious enough to add an Italianate mansard crown and a gallery or two or three. Later owners planted patios leading to formal gardens and the end result is stunning, made even more attractive by the tender lovin' care and good taste exhibited by Clark, as evidenced in both the private and public rooms.

The fireplace in the downstairs sitting room beckons on chilly evenings, and on lazy summer days there is a croquet court and chairs for breathing in the country air out front. The rooms are handsomely furnished, with canopy beds and four-posters, with fine carpets and the original hardware on doors and windows. I especially like the third floor two-bedroom suite with beautiful period furniture, a private bath and views of the countryside and the tow path along the Delaware.

Except for a Continental breakfast featuring freshly baked delights, there is no meal service at the Woolverton. But that is no problem in this area with so many inns and restaurants on both sides of the river. On the Jersey side, there is the Sergeantsville Inn, a perfectly preserved eighteenth-century provincial stone house two and one-half miles northeast on State Road 523, which is also the site of the only covered bridge still standing in the state. Partners John Touhey and Frank Ayres do wondrous things, changing menus every two months, and featuring festive dinners, suppers and brunches during the holiday season. To stimulate the appetite, consider their grilled swordfish, which they marinate first in peanut oil showered with garlic, ginger, sesame seeds and soy sauce; their chicken breast stuffed with mushroom duxelle and cheddar cheese and surrounded by bacon; the shrimp sautéed with basil, capers, garlic, tomato bits and onions swimming in white wine; the pork chops refreshed with a strawberry-rhubarb sauce. The Woolverton, complemented by the Sergeantsville Inn, provides reason enough for never crossing the river.

THE WOOLVERTON INN, R.D. 3, Box 233-A, Stockton, New Jersey 08559. Telephone: (609) 397-0802. Accommodations: ten rooms; shared baths; one suite with private bath; no telephones; television in public room. Rates: moderate, includes complimentary Continental breakfast and afternoon tea. No young children. No pets. Cards: AE. Open all year.

Getting There: The inn is three-tenths of a mile from the intersection of State Roads 29 and 523 in Stockton and one-tenth of a mile off 523; take the second drive on the right.

A Castagna Creation of Great Style

CHESTNUT HILL ON THE DELAWARE

Milford, New Jersey

There is a wrought iron, lacey, Louisiana-lazy look to this 1860 Victorian dominating a slope overlooking the banks of the Delaware. Built for the young bride of one Wilson Thomas, it went through its first 122 years in the hands of Thomas and his descendents and then just one other family until Linda and Rob Castagna took over in 1982. They found a home that had been lovingly, fussily cared for, and they quickly worked the transformation of family home into a bed and breakfast inn of great charm and grand style.

The Castagnas were not content to cash in on the work of others, however. They approach their innkeeping responsibilities with too much dedication to relax into that kind of escape. Rob put up some forty rolls of wallpaper in the third floor suite, called "Teddy's Place" and containing a pair of bedrooms that could accommodate a family or two couples traveling together, and an Italian-tiled bath that looks through neo-Italianate windows to the river. He also did the gold leaf overlay along the molding in the gallery of a drawing room which is

Chestnut Hill on the Delaware

complete with pump organ and boldly Victorian furnishings—Eastlake design of black walnut—and the kind of potted greenery, crocheted table runners and arm covers to complement perfectly the turn-of-the-century ambiance. Linda's little gift baskets, some local pottery and imports from Wales and England, and an assortment of other suitably sweet items are on view in the gallery, including the English soaps found in the rooms. There is the Pineapple Room, a junior suite with a television tucked away and a delightful white pedestal shell sink, in the former servant's quarters. The Peaches and Cream Room and the Bayberry Room reflect their names and provide a sophisticated country escape from the real world.

Castagna's superlative creation is the northern outpost of all the inns, converted barns, ancient taverns and stone mansions and all the history that follows the Delaware River on both the Jersey and Pennsylvania sides from the site of General George Washington's famous Christmas crossing in the south, through New Hope and Lambertville and all the way to Upper Black Eddy and Chestnut Hill.

CHESTNUT HILL ON THE DELAWARE, 63 Church Street (P.O. Box N), Milford, New Jersey 08848. Telephone: (210) 995-9761. Accommodations: two rooms and two suites; suites with private baths; no telephones; one suite with television. Rates: moderate to expensive, includes complimentary breakfast. Inquire about children. No pets. No cards. No smoking. Open all year.

Getting There: Follow Church Street one block from the bridge to the inn, which is the last house on the left-hand side.

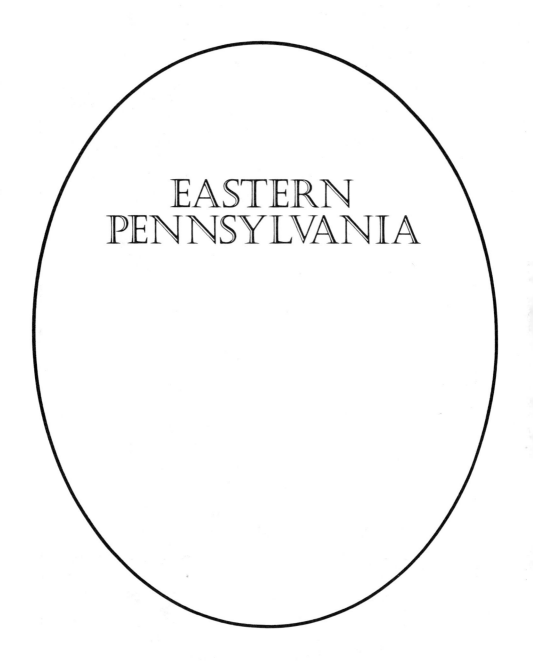

EASTERN
PENNSYLVANIA

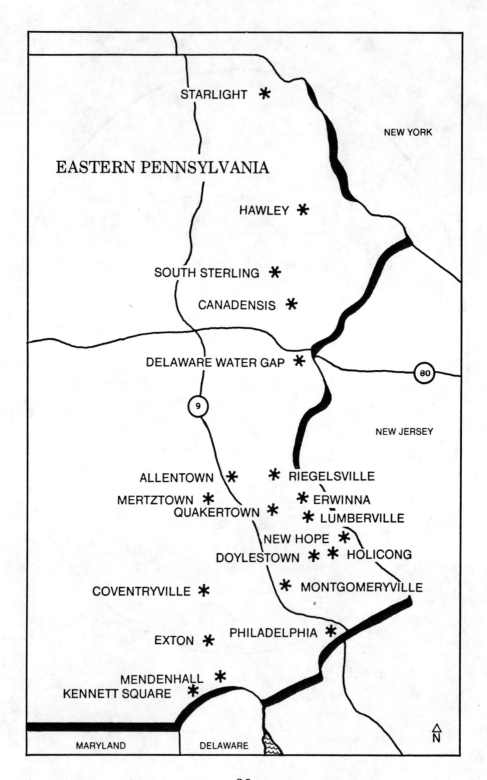

EASTERN PENNSYLVANIA

STARLIGHT *

NEW YORK

HAWLEY *

SOUTH STERLING *

CANADENSIS *

DELAWARE WATER GAP *

(80)

(9)

NEW JERSEY

ALLENTOWN * * RIEGELSVILLE

MERTZTOWN * * ERWINNA

QUAKERTOWN * * LUMBERVILLE

NEW HOPE *

DOYLESTOWN * * HOLICONG

COVENTRYVILLE * * MONTGOMERYVILLE

PHILADELPHIA *

EXTON *

MENDENHALL *
KENNETT SQUARE *

N

MARYLAND   DELAWARE

SOUTHEASTERN
PENNSYLVANIA

Best Act in Berks County
BLAIR CREEK INN
Mertztown, Pennsylvania

Blair Henry and his partner Jim are the main men at this class act of the county. They transformed an 1847 Quaker Meeting House into a jewel of a restaurant, wallpapering one room with 108 menus, putting upholstered high-back chairs in another that they labeled the San Francisco Room. My favorite sitting here is at the table for two by the window overlooking the beautiful gardens with gazebo—a most romantic setting.

The food here established the reputation. Blair, graduate of Paris' Cordon Bleu, oversees an international menu, one complemented with a good wine cellar. Appetizers range from humus served with pita to shrimp-pineapple stuffed avocado, from fresh chicken livers sautéed with a Madeira-spiked sauce to giant mushroom caps overflowing with lump crabmeal. Entrées can be as uncomplicated as a rack of lamb, Chateaubriand bouquetière and pepper steak, or as involved as blending clams, oysters and chicken breast in a crock and coating it with buttered bread crumbs before baking, or tangling Portuguese calamari and New England clams with freshly made pasta. These selections, always served with three vegetables and followed by stunning desserts, are from a fall and winter menu. Warmer weather brings lighter fare. And each Sunday brings a brunch that should be the envy of most far more famous establishments. It has become so popular, in part because it is a sit-down-waiter-served affair, that reservations are required.

Reservations are also required for accommodations in the beautifully restored 1814 barn at the back of the property. Mini-suites, one called Loft and the other Stable, are plushly furnished and have working fireplaces. Views from the windows are sensational, overlooking gardens where flowers are found in abundance—and there is always a mass of fresh flowers in the inn, along with strawberries. This is a hallmark of this special place: fresh strawberries every day of the year.

BLAIR CREEK INN, Mertztown, Pennsylvania19539. Telephone: (215) 682-4201. Accommodations: two suites; private baths; telephones; televisions. Rates: expensive, includes Continental breakfast. No children. No pets. Cards: AE, MC, VISA. Open all year.

Getting There: From Allentown follow U.S. 222 (Hamilton Street) west to Trexlertown, crossing over State Road 100; continue for 3.7 miles, take a left turn into Mertztown and from there continue 2.1 miles to a stop sign; turn left and then left again at the next stop sign; continue 1.2 miles to the inn, which is 1.4 miles from the post office in the center of town.

The Food Alone is Worth the Trip
SIGN OF THE SORREL HORSE
Quakertown, Pennsylvania

Isolated in a bucolic setting just north of Lake Nockamixon and its state park, perfect for canoeing, fishing, swimming and hiking (with box lunches provided by the inn), this sweetly appointed hideaway with its antique furnishings is a good escape destination for Philadelphians wanting to get away from it all. It is also a worthwhile base camp for antique hunters—there are dozens of dealers in the immediate area.

An inn since the time of the American Revolution, it is another of the many hostelries frequented by early stagecoach travelers and its origins are clearly and cleanly exposed by the modern innkeepers. There are thick fieldstone walls, hand-cut beams and timbers, wide-board pine flooring and low windows, all lending to a great sense of place.

Fresh fruit and flowers greet the guest on arrival and there is sherry and reading material in the common room leading to the private accommodations, a swimming pool, well-manicured grounds and world class cheffing.

The softly lighted dining room—magnet for many who come from miles around—features superb food. In a striking display of culinary virtuosity, the kitchen produces excellent fish soup spiked with garlic, oysters wrapped in grape leaves heightened with lemon and caviar and a parade of pâtés and terrines. Entrées range from steamed turbans of salmon and sole to ginger chicken en papillote, marinated lamb brochettes on tomato pasta to a breast of duck glazed with honey and presented with a poached pear, and fresh rainbow trout with a hazelnut mousse to prime veal sautéed with roasted shallots splashed with cassis.

THE SIGN OF THE SORREL HORSE, Old Bethlehem Road, Quakertown, Pennsylvania 18951. Telephone: (215) 536-4651. Accommodations: six rooms; private baths; no telephones; no televisions. Rates: moderate, includes Continental breakfast. Children and pets not permitted. Cards: AE, DC, MC, VISA. Open all year.

Getting There: From Philadelphia take State Road 309 north to State Road 563 and then north for seven miles to Old Bethlehem Road; turn left and proceed 1/4 mile to the inn.

Everything But a Coach
COACHAUS
Allentown, Pennsylvania

"In the evening, after you have slain your dragons (or come home wounded), we welcome you with understanding. Our guests are welcome at our traditional 'attitude adjustment hour,' the civilized way to end a day when you are away from home." So reads the charmingly composed brochure advertising the attractions of this inn which is so convenient to the stores and restaurants of town, a half block from the Olde Allentown Historical District.

Each of the rooms, the suites and full-fledged apartments is individually decorated, displaying considerable taste and restraint, with some antiques, coordinated fabrics and comfy beds, plus all the modern amenities. And for those guests touring and/or working for extended periods of time, the innkeeper arranges for maid service and laundry, and will be happy to assist in providing information on the locations of attractions in the general area. For something special in Allentown, check in for one of their "Royal Weekends," built around fresh fruit and flowers, champagne, and brunch in the mornings.

COACHAUS, 107–111 North Eighth Street, Allentown, Pennsylvania 18102. Telephone: (215) 821-4854. Accommodations: 12 rooms, suites and apartments; private baths; telephones; televisions. Rates: moderate to expensive, includes full breakfast. Children and pets permitted. Cards: AE, MC, VISA. Open all year.

Getting There: From U.S. 22 exit at Seventh Street and go 1.5 miles south to Linden Street; turn right and right again at the next street which is Eighth. The inn is near the corner, on the right hand side of the street.

Tote That Barge
RIEGELSVILLE HOTEL
Riegelsville, Pennsylvania

Another one of the many hostelries hugging the Delaware River, built in the nineteenth century when that watery artery and its canals were major transportation routes. The spirit of those days survives in this white blockhouse with red trim shutters and its handsome dining room dotted with islands of stiff white napery and its china sporting designs recalling the old canal boat days, catching the light from a glistening teardrop chandelier. The high back Windsor chairs are comfort plus, and the back room provides a meal that is as honest as the setting: duckling, strip steaks, shrimps tangled with mushrooms, a heavenly oyster-parmesan.

Guestrooms are not elaborate; in fact this is very definitely the least formal, most relaxed and rustic of the many inns of the New Hope area. Innkeepers Fran and Harry Cregar, who live on the second floor of the hotel, want to keep it that way—and so does their son, Harry, who is in charge of the back room. He also was the one who did the "jugenstil," art nouveau stained glass panels in the dining room. They are especially attractive at night during colder months when the two fireplaces in the dining room are blazing.

RIEGELSVILLE HOTEL, 10 Delaware Road, Riegelsville, Pennsylvania 18077. Telephone: (215) 749-2469. Accommodations: 12 rooms; five private baths; no telephones or televisions. Full bar service; lunch and dinner served. Children welcome. No pets. Cards: MC, VISA. Open all year.

Getting There: Delaware Road is at the traffic light eight miles south of Easton along River Road off State Road 611; go over the narrow bridge just before the main bridge over the Delaware River.

Ever Elegant
EVER MAY ON THE DELAWARE
Erwinna, Pennsylvania

In a picture postcard perfect setting surrounded by twenty-five acres of tended woods and gardens embracing the canal, this three-story jewel sparkles with the painstaking restoration efforts of its owners who opened this inn's doors to the public in March 1983. The first room seen by the arriving guest, perhaps a trifle overwhelmed by the circular drive approach and the tranquility all about, is the living room with its baby grand, a pair of fireplaces, grandfather clock and decanter of sherry.

From that enclave of elegance, one proceeds to the perfectly furnished guest rooms, some with fireplaces. My favorite has a sleigh bed in a sitting room. In a separate carriage house, also beautifully revitalized, there are two ground floor rooms and a suite on the second floor with two bedrooms, sitting room and bath, ideal for a family or two couples traveling together. Fresh fruit, plants and flowers greet each guest, and there is tea at four in the parlour and sherry in the evening.

The oldest part of the inn dates from the early eighteenth century. In 1871 additions were made when the structure was renovated and converted into a rather elegant hotel, which lasted until the Great Depression. After overnighting one beautiful fall day at Ever May, I have trouble believing it ever was more elegant—in a restrained Bucks County kind of way—than it is at present.

On weekends, five-course dinners are served at 7:30 and excellent breakfasts are available every day of the week. The morning meal is taken in the conservatory, a glassed-in back porch, bright yellow and beckoning to the wildlife outside. In the course of consuming a beautifully presented fruit cup (all fresh of course), blueberry and strawberry cream cheese beignets and excellent coffee, I saw some deer, a miniflock of mallards, peacocks and even a few goats and sheep.

It was extremely hard to leave that bucolic scene, but I knew I would be returning. Ever May is one of my favorite escapes anywhere in this book.

EVER MAY ON THE DELAWARE, River Road (State Road 32), Erwinna, Pennsylvania 18920. Telephone: (215) 294-9100. Accommodations: 16 rooms; private baths; no telephones; no televisions. Rates: moderate to expensive, includes Continental breakfast. Children and pets not permitted. Cards: MC, VISA. Open all year.

Everything's Pleasant With This Pheasant
GOLDEN PHEASANT INN
Erwinna, Pennsylvania

The basic building has been serving as hostelry and hugging the shores of the Delaware Canal and River since 1857. That was when some 2,500 barges were regularly making the run between Bristol and Easton, carrying coal and limestone. The structure was restored in 1967 and, not long after, the owners also transformed an older building to inn: the Federal-style Stover Mansion, a few minutes away and built in 1834.

Three of its eight guest rooms have fireplaces and there is a marvelous living room for lounging. All of the woodwork in the three-story Mansion with mansard roof is cherry, milled and cut at the sawmill owned by Stover. There are six guest rooms in the inn and each is individually decorated, each with an antique bed and an ambiance befitting the memories of this old structure.

Alongside is the greenhouse of a dining room, replete with plants and formal table appointments, including pheasant service plates, of course. Food at the glittering pheasant is international, with seasonal shifts on the menu; but they usually try to have pheasant on the bill of fare, along with duckling à l'orange, chicken in a restrained curry sauce, charbroiled steaks (and sometimes venison steaks), marinated beef in a peanut sauce, and sweetbreads in a light cream sauce spiked with port.

For diners wishing a more intimate setting for such notable food, there is the inside dining room with plush love seats and Tiffany lighting, and during the summer months courtship should commence on the porch, seated on wicker and sipping a bit of the bubbly.

GOLDEN PHEASANT INN, River Road, Erwinna, Pennsylvania 18920. Telephone: (215) 294-9595. Accommodations: 14 rooms; shared baths; no telephones; no televisions. Rates: moderate, includes Continental breakfast. Children permitted No pets. Cards: AE, VISA. Open mid-February through mid-December.

Getting There: The inn is 17 miles north of New Hope on State Road 32.

BLACK BASS HOTEL

Lumberville, Pennsylvania

A bit of bonnie Britain whose owners and most of its clientele remained loyal to the King during the revolution, this historic hostelry, which has served canal and river passengers along the Delaware since the 1740s, is a vibrant, vital echo of the past. I really do have the feeling that a Tory is going to walk in while I'm standing at that splendid pewter bar, surrounded by royal portraits and scenes that might grace any earl's estate in Mother England. Or while I'm seated at one of those unique dining room tables made from old slaughtering surfaces and ringed by chairs of every description.

And what a dining room it is, when crowded with happy faces filling themselves with the imaginative outpourings from the back room: pheasant soup, oysters en brochette, avocado stuffed with crab for starters; followed by the house specialty of Charleston Meeting Street

44

Crabmeat, shrimp and mushrooms sautéed in garlic butter, veal scallops enhanced by a burgundy pâté sauce or roast duck Normandy. For finishers there are deep dish apple pie, rum cream pie, pecan crunch and, in season, marvelous pumpkin pie spiked with apple jack and dolloped with whipped cream that never saw the inside of a can. When I last worked through such a menu, I complemented it with a bottle from Bucks County Vineyards, a one hundred-percent Pennsylvania product which, if not quite "reminiscent of most famous wines of Bordeaux," as the label promised, was surprisingly good, ruby red in color and pleasantly dry to the taste.

I had the same favorable reaction to the breads, made with unbleached white flour, bran and whole wheat, and I was impressed with the pleasantness and professionalism of the serving staff.

The guest rooms on the second floor of this vest-pocket hotel are furnished in Colonial style, in keeping with the spirit of the place, although one of the bedsteads is pure Victorian. Several of them have a balcony surrounded by a cast-iron balustrade which races across the back, providing a lacy framework for the wonderful views of the river and canal. They are perfect retreats for breakfast at the right time of the year.

BLACK BASS HOTEL, Route 32 (River Road), Lumberville, Pennsylvania 18933. Telephone: (215) 297-5815. Accommodations: seven rooms sharing bath and two-bedroom suite with private bath; no telephones; no televisions. Rates: moderate to expensive, includes Continental breakfast. No children. No pets. Cards: AE, MC, VISA. Open all year.

Getting There: The inn is eight miles north of New Hope on State Road 32, River Road.

Peaceful Retreat with Taste
1740 HOUSE
Lumberville, Pennsylvania

There is no history of famous patriots or other illustrious personages who have overnighted here, but owners Janet and Harry Nessler have produced a perfect country inn, nestled in the trees and overlooking the Delaware River and Canal with its towpath that is ideal for energetic hiking or leisurely strolling. A swimming pool is on the premises and close by is the spread of restaurants, shops, galleries and more inns, seven miles away in New Hope.

The two dozen rooms that ramble lazily from the central structure, an old stable with exposed beams and rugged stone walls, have terraces overlooking this restful scene, and the small dining room (dinner reservations required, for inn guests as well as general public) is glassed in to allow diners to continue enjoying the view.

The menu is not large and it is primarily Continental in scope; at breakfast there is a generously stocked buffet for do-it-yourself early morning nourishment. There is no liquor license, but setups are provided and nearby wine stores can supply the bottles for the B.Y.O.B. policy.

1740 HOUSE, River Road, Lumberville, Pennsylvania 18933. Telephone: (215) 297-5661. Accommodations: 24 rooms; private baths; no telephones; no televisions. Rates: moderate, includes Continental breakfast. Children permitted. No pets. No cards. Open all year.

Getting There: The inn is on State Road 32 N (River Road), seven miles from New Hope.

1740 House

Williamsburg on the Delaware
CENTRE BRIDGE INN
New Hope, Pennsylvania

One of the best times to come to this re-creation of something special farther south—all the way to Williamsburg, Virginia—is during the summer, when meals can be eaten on the patio which has a spectacular view of the Delaware River and Canal, where mule-drawn barges glide past. The barges run from April through October and during this period New Hope—with its Bucks County Playhouse, State Theater of Pennsylvania, artists' colony and its many shops, galleries, restaurants and inns as easy to recommend as this one—is usually bumper to bumper, elbow to elbow. And this is especially true on weekends.

This is why the accommodations, the tranquil escapes, are important. And that is why I like the Centre Bridge. It combines the best of two worlds: the modern comforts of today and the sense of the past. Each room is color-coordinated in a quiet, non-splashy manner with quilt-covered brass and four-poster canopy beds. My favorite room is Number 9, with its four-poster canopy, cedar-lined bathroom, and private terrace overlooking the river, the towpath below beckoning me to take a stroll.

My favorite meal in the tavern-like lower level dining room, which has a marvelous bar tucked into one corner, heavy overhead beams and a giant stone fireplace, begins with a shrimp and lobster mousseline served with a light fish velout. Then calves' liver sautéd with shallots and onions in white wine and fond de vaulie, a steak marchand du vin, or a rack of lamb roasted with breadcrumbs dijonaise then glazed with a mint-enhanced béarnaise.

There is a fine wine list, along with a piano quietly playing in the background, a dramatic use of candles and masses of flowers, creating the ultimate in romantic settings. Another plus signifying the intelligence of the management at Centre Bridge: cigar and pipe smoking is permitted only at the bar, not at the tables.

The same applies at breakfast when guests gather in a little tavern that looks as though it is on the guided tour of Colonial Williamsburg. The last time I sat there one crisp fall day I compared notes with the other inn guests and quickly learned that each couple was planning to do something quite different. The elderly couple was going to check out all the covered bridges in Bucks County. There are thirteen of them (out of the original 36) and they had a little flyer detailing their trip which was to start at the Memorial Building at Washington Crossing State Park where there is a fine copy of the famous painting depicting the dramatic Christmas crossing. Another couple intended to start walking the towpath of the canal—it runs some sixty miles, from Bristol to Easton and is known as Roosevelt State Park. Another planned to ride on the barge, and a young twosome wanted to visit Pearl Buck's home, now a National Historic Landmark, along with other historic houses in the area: Hulmeville, first home of painter Edward Hicks, and the several ancient buildings in Fallsington where there are guided tours from March 15 to November 15.

CENTRE BRIDGE INN, River Road (P.O. Box 74), Star Route, New Hope, Pennsylvania 18938. Telephone: (215) 862-2048. Accommodations: nine rooms; private baths; no telephones; some rooms with televisions. Rates: moderate to expensive. "Well behaved children only, no infants." No pets. Cards: MC, VISA. Open all year.

Getting There: The inn is 3.3 miles south of New Hope's only traffic light on State Road 32, River Road, at the intersection with State Road 263.

Prime Location
THE WEDGWOOD INN
New Hope, Pennsylvania

This 1870 Victorian mansion has been a guest house since 1950, but not until present owners Nadine Silnutzer and Carl Glassman took over a decade later did it begin to glisten from TLC and an array of interesting antiques, including a namesake collection of Wedgwood. Brass and spool beds covered with old quilts, a converted foot-pedal sewing machine, paddle fans, oriental rugs, sideboards, and the smell of fresh-baked bread each morning are some of the extras in this immaculately maintained home away from home. There are fresh flowers in all the rooms and, at night, a carafe of Amaretto and turned-down beds with a chocolate on the pillow.

Carl, the baker, does wonders with the morning muffins, croissants, and breads, which are served with fresh-squeezed orange juice and mounds of freshly assembled fruit and strong, bracing coffee. This can be consumed in the spacious guest rooms, on the sun porch, or, ideally, in the Victorian gazebo on bright spring, summer or fall mornings.

And in the living room is a library of information on all there is to see and do in a county which has fascinated city dwellers ever since Colonial days. The inn is perfectly situated for strolling the streets of the Historic District. While there, check into the New Hope Information Center on the corner of South Main and Mechanic Streets. They will be able to provide everything—and probably more—that you ever wanted to know about an area that has attractions ranging from a Washington Crossing the Delaware Park to auto and antique shows.

THE WEDGWOOD INN, 111 West Bridge Street, New Hope, Pennsylvania 18938. Telephone: (215) 862-2570. Accommodations: 10 rooms; eight private baths; public telephone; no televisions. Rates: moderate, includes Continental breakfast. Children permitted. No pets. No cards. Open all year.

Getting There: The inn occupies a prominence in the New Hope Historic District two blocks south of the Lambertville Bridge on West Bridge Street.

A Place to Pig Out

INN AT PHILLIPS MILL
New Hope, Pennsylvania

The Copper Pig hanging over the entrance to this total encapsulation of charm is surely the best-known sign in Bucks County, if not the state. It signifies the fact that next door to this one-time stable there once was a piggery. Both buildings, along with a grist mill powered by the waters of the Delaware, were put up on one of the grand pre-Revolutionary estates in the 1750s. The stone structure, with its low ceilings, spacious fireplaces (one faced by an oversize leather couch), and collection of old plates and curious artifacts with a pig now and then, looks as though it will last another two hundred years.

Flowers, fresh and dried, are artistically arranged in the several dining areas where the food delivered is as captivating as the setting. Especially when one starts a summer meal with cold strawberry soup or a lightly tossed scallop salad, or in colder months when the fireplaces blaze away, something heavier: tournedos with artichoke hearts and béarnaise honoring Henri IV, chicken breasts, a pepper steak, Dover sole, duckling inspired by a Grand Marnier sauce with the added zing of lemon-lime, a steamed vegetable platter, and of course something from the piggery—pork chops with prunes.

Public and private rooms are small, but somehow the designers made them seem spacious, even in a small upstairs guest room under the eaves. However, that room is not recommended for basketball players. They would have considerable trouble avoiding the rafters while leaping out of bed to retrieve the basket of breakfast left outside each morning by innkeepers Brooks and Joyce Kaufman.

INN AT PHILLIPS MILL, North River Road (State Road 32), New Hope, Pennsylvania 18938. Telephone: (215) 862-2984. Accommodations: five rooms; private baths; no telephones; no televisions. Rates: moderate. Children permitted. No pets. No cards. Open all year except for six weeks during January and February.

Getting There: The inn is located 1.5 miles north of New Hope on State Road 32, North River Road.

BARLEY SHEAF FARM
Holicong, Pennsylvania

Drive under the tall maples and enter into another world: a country estate that is on the National Register of Historic Places. A pastoral retreat where, in loyalty to its name, there actually are horses and sheep, pigs and chickens, and a little pond dotted with ducks and geese. There is also a swimming pool—one of the oldest in the county—croquet and badminton courts, and thirty acres of spacious land to wander, watching the animals.

The rooms, in the main house and a nearby cottage, are very well maintained and furnished with a grand variety of antiques. My favorite is the suite, complete with queen-size bed, a fireplace and trundle bed if desired for those traveling with wee ones—but not under the age of eight, the innkeepers advise. Over that age, children should find the farm exposure rather educational as well as entertaining.

Accommodations here always include a bountiful farm-style breakfast, and that means fresh eggs from some of those clucking hens, honey made from their own hives, scrapple and sausage and bread baked by Ann Mills, who with husband Don, is responsible for this peaceful refuge so near and yet so far from all the activity of New Hope. That is probably why playwright George S. Kaufman chose to buy the house and live under the maples and copper beeches for so many years.

This farmhouse has it all: history—the origins go back to 1740— rural escape, the vibes of Kaufman and his cronies the Marx Brothers, friendly innkeepers and wonderful country food.

BARLEY SHEAF FARM, P.O. Box 10 Route 202, Holicong, Pennsylvania 18928. Telephone: (215) 794-5104. Accommodations: nine rooms; seven private baths; no telephones; no televisions. Rates: moderate to expensive, includes full breakfast. Children under 8 not advised and pets not permitted. No cards. Open March 1 to Christmas.

Getting There: The inn is about midway between Buckingham and Iahaska on State Road 202.

The Miracles of Mercer
DOYLESTOWN INN
Doylestown, Pennsylvania

Here is the perfect headquarters for anyone wanting to pay homage to one of Pennsylvania's super achievers, Henry Chapman Mercer. A Doylestown native, in three-quarters of a century (he died in 1930), he made major, seminal contributions to archaeology and anthropology, the study of handicrafts and early American agricultural implements, as well as to the manufacture of tile, pottery and mosaics.

His many accomplishments are on public display in what the locals proudly refer to as The Mercer Mile, three concrete extravaganzas: his cement castle home, Fonthill, the Moravian Pottery and Tile Works where tiles are still being produced according to the Mercer method, and the Mercer Museum with the Spruance Library on Bucks County history and genealogy. There are more than forty thousand objects and the tools of over forty crafts at the museum.

The museum is only a few blocks from the Doylestown Inn, the castle and manufactory about a mile away. And the walk to them is along the lanes of a quiet little Main Street kind of town, as typical of small town America as the inn, built in 1902. There is a homey charm about both the guestrooms and the public rooms, one called Publick Tavern, another the Jug in the Wall Tavern, with live entertainment. Among the specialties are the boneless breast of chicken rolled in chopped walnuts and coated with a brandy-spiked cream sauce, the "chain-gang chili" with its shower of grated Swiss cheese and chopped onions and freshly baked pies and brownies "à la James Beard."

DOYLESTOWN INN, 18 West State Street, Doylestown, Pennsylvania 18901. Telephone: (215) 345-6610. Accommodations: 22 rooms; private baths; telephones; television. Rates: inexpensive. Full bar and meal service. Children permitted. No pets. Cards: AE, DC, MC, VISA. Open all year.

Getting There: Doylestown is 12 miles from New Hope, Pennsylvania at the intersection of U.S. 611 and 202; the inn is in the center of the town on its main east-west artery.

Amble On In
JOSEPH AMBLER INN
Montgomeryville, Pennsylvania

Far from the madding crowd clustered in and close to New Hope, this bucolic retreat provides the visitor to the valley with an abundance of history (it is nineteen miles from Valley Forge), a country estate kind of quiet and a twelve-acre refuge with finesse and more than a few touches of old-fashioned charm. The rooms and suites are handsomely outfitted with antique furniture, four-poster beds, oriental rugs, carefully co-ordinated drapes, coverlets and wall coverings, and each is named for a famed Pennsylvania personage, including William Penn and Joseph Ambler.

Ambler was the name chosen for the inn when it was opened in 1982. He was a skilled eighteenth-century wheelwright and he built this home in the country in 1734. The present caretakers, those who so carefully restored and revitalized this grand old building, were loyal to his high standards of construction. They also refurnished an adjoining school room with a gigantic walk-in fireplace. It is now used for conferences and small meetings.

JOSEPH AMBLER INN, 1005 Horsham Road, Montgomeryville, Pennsylvania 19454. Telephone: (215) 362-7500. Accommodations: 15 rooms and suites; private baths; televisions; telephones. Rates: moderate to expensive, includes breakfast. Children under 12 and pets not permitted. Cards: AE, MC, VISA. Open all year.

Joseph Ambler Inn

Getting There: From the Fort Washington Exit of the Pennsylvania pike drive north seven miles on State Road 309 to the second traffic light; turn right onto Stump Road and then left onto Horsham Road—inn is on the right.

Ultimate Urban Inn
SOCIETY HILL HOTEL
Philadelphia, Pennsylvania

A beautifully revitalized solidly built four-story structure, built in 1832 and reborn in 1981, the year before Philadelphia celebrated its three hundredth anniversary, this inn is ideally located for all those who want to take a time capsule blast into the past. Smack in the center of Independence National Historical Park, it is across the street from the Visitors Center where there is a fine film about the importance of this City of Brotherly Love, and its role in the American Revolution. The cobblestone alleys you walk were trod by the founding fathers, and in Carpenter's Hall the First Continental Congress was assembled in 1774. Independence Hall, familiar to any school child, towers over the scene and there are beautifully restored Colonial taverns, a glass pavilion housing the cracked Liberty Bell, and a museum detailing the many incredible achievements of Benjamin Franklin.

After all that history, after that crash course in the courageous actions of our Colonial fathers, there is no more fitting retreat to consider and contemplate the past than the Society Hill Hotel. The rooms are comfortable, overflowing with Federal touches and historic reminders: crown moulding, stencils, brass beds and antiques intermingled with more modern pieces.

And each morning the breakfast tray arrives with its freshly squeezed orange juice, coffeecake or croissants, fresh fruit, coffee or tea; a "Continental tradition with an American flair," as innkeepers Thomas Kleinman, David DeGraff and Judith Campbell describe it. It makes a great start to a day of still more immersion in Philadelphia's past.

SOCIETY HILL HOTEL, 301 Chestnut Street, Philadelphia, Pennsylvania 19106. Telephone: (215) 925-1394. Accommodations: 12 rooms; private baths; telephones and televisions. Rates: moderate, includes

Continental breakfast. Full bar and restaurant. Children permitted. No pets. Cards: AE, MC, VISA. Open all year.

Getting There: Chestnut Street is between Third and Fourth Streets.

Sightseeing Headquarters
MENDENHALL INN
Mendenhall, Pennsylvania

There is so much to see in this immediate area—as detailed in the review of Longwood Inn—that one should really consider checking into this modernized country inn for a week. That would give the visitor ample time to give such sensational happenings as Winterthur their just due and leave time enough for the many other museums, especially for the stunningly beautiful Longwood Gardens.

The rooms are simply furnished, each of them with comfortable double beds, and there is a restaurant serving lunch and dinner at prices as moderate as the rooms; in fact the tariffs represent some of the better bargains in the area.

For other inn eating in this section of the state, search out Chadds Ford Inn in the town of the same name. The building dates from 1703 and the chef shows considerable imagination. The Marshallton Inn on State Road 162 in Marshallton has been feeding tourists since the eighteenth century and current accents there are French.

MENDENHALL INN, Kenneth Pike, Route 52 (P.O. Box 208), Mendenhall, Pennsylvania 19357. Telephone: (215) 388-1181. Accommodations: 21 rooms; private baths; no televisions. Rates: moderate. Children permitted. No pets. Cards: MC, VISA. Open all year.

Getting There: The inn is on the main street of the village, State Road 52.

LONGWOOD INN
Kennett Square, Pennsylvania

Renovated and refurbished in 1983, this easy-to-recommend base camp for exploring the many must-see attractions of the area has a restaurant that specializes in the prime product of the area: mushrooms. Kennett Square calls itself the Mushroom Capital of the United States. The Longwood Inn's mushroom soup is delicious, but then so is their cream of crab imperial and, on weekends, they feature live Maine lobster. Always available are their Pennsylvania Dutch specialties: apple dumplings and Lancaster County ham steak with a raisin sauce.

The family responsible for so much good food is the Skiadas clan, who also operate the Family Style, Amish Barn and Windmill restaurants in Lancaster County. They were hardly beginners when they took over the Longwood, revitalizing the grand old Colonial brick building tucked into a spread of carefully manicured landscaping.

Guest rooms, comfortably furnished, are also carefully maintained and are welcome retreats after a day of sight seeing.

Longwood Gardens, 350 acres of eye-popping blooms and trees with 14,000 different kinds of plants, outdoor theater and super-size pipe organ, is only a half mile away. The Brandywine River Museum is four jiles distant as is the Hillendale Museum. The Hagley Museum and the Delaware Museum of Natural History are only six miles away and the incredible Winterthur is a mere seven. And Longwood Inn is close to Pennsylvania's Horse Country, so don't be too surprised when you see the steeplechase riders leaping the fences lacing the beautiful countryside.

LONGWOOD INN, 815 East Baltimore Pike, Kennett Square, Pennsylvania 19348. Telephone: (215) 444-3515. Accommodations: 28 rooms; private baths; telephones; televisions. Rates: moderate. Children welcome. No pets. Cards: AE, CB, DC, MC, VISA. Open all year.

Getting There: The inn is on U.S. 1, a few minutes northeast of the center of town.

DULING KURTZ HOUSE AND COUNTRY INN
Exton, Pennsylvania

The Duling and Kurtz names honor the mothers of the founders of this inn, on property that was once part of a land grant by William Penn. In the 1830s there were a grist and saw mill, log tenement, lime kilns and limestone quarries on the land, along with the solid stone structure which now serves as inn. Later owners of the land included the great grandfather of Vice President Hubert Humphrey and a remarkable woman, Martha Gibbons Thomas, member of Bryn Mawr's first graduating class in 1899. She was a prominent suffragette and cattle breeder who was one of the first eight women elected to Pennsylvania's House of Representatives, serving from 1922 to 1926.

But her name is not included in the roster of distinguished Americans (plus Winston Churchill) whose names have been selected for the eighteen guest rooms. Dolly Madison and Susan B. Anthony and Betsy Ross did make the cut, however. As did Washington and Lincoln of course. The Washington room is large, with a king-size, high-posted cherry canopy bed and a step-down bath; that named for the Great Emancipator has a sitting room with sofa bed and twin canopy beds and a private courtyard. Behind the Booker T. Washington nameplate is a double bed and another private courtyard and in both the Thomas Jefferson and Franklin D. Roosevelt rooms there are fireplaces. One room has a queen-size poster bed, the other a cannonball bed. Some guests specify in advance which room they want to stay in, thus identifying with a particular patriot, and I wish they had a Teddy Roosevelt room complete with animal heads on the walls and a little bear by the bed.

However, I'll settle for one of the rooms with private courtyard, and to continue the insulation from other guests, I'll reserve the special private dining room (for two or four) tucked into a corner of the inn's stunning restaurant. The menu can be preselected, but the choice is not an easy one. How to decide between carpaccio reposing on a dill-mustard sauce sprinkled with parmesan and pepper, and chilled poached salmon nestled neatly on a bed of spinach fettuccine heightened by a basil vinaigrette? Or entrées which include medallions of lobster sautéed with snow peas and chanterelles suspended in saffron sauce, fillets of pork tangled with apples and Shiitake mushrooms finished with Calvados, or a veal chop sautéed with shallots and sun-dried tomatoes enhanced with just the right touch of garlic? The baked-out-back breads and the salads, including spinach leaves tossed with a whole mustard seed dressing, and a radicchio-romaine combination showered with pine nuts and alfalfa sprouts suspended in a dill-basil vinaigrette, are as outstanding as the freshly made desserts and their own special ice cream. Few of the famous Americans honored in this elegant inn ever ate this well.

DULING KURTZ HOUSE AND COUNTRY INN, South Whitford Road, Exton, Pennsylvania 19341. Telephone: (215) 524-1830. Accommodations: 18 rooms; private baths; telephones; televisions. Rates: expensive, including Continental breakfast. Children under 12 and pets not permitted. Cards: AE, MC, VISA. Open all year.

Getting There: Exton is located at the intersection of U.S. 30 and State Road 100; the inn is impossible to miss in the village.

Haute Cuisine in the Hills
COVENTRY FORGE INN
Coventryville, Pennsylvania

Would you believe crème de cresson, feuilleté d'Escargots champenoise, saumon troisgros, ris de veau au madère, and profiteroles glacé in a country inn built fifteen years before George Washington was born? These are just a few of the strictly French surprises on the menu in this most ancient of country hideaways, built as a chestnut log home, now covered with white stucco, and housing one of the best dining rooms in this book. Actually, there are two dining rooms, beautifully paneled in pine, one left bare and the other, the one with the old Franklin stove worked into the fireplace, painted in reds. The one-time kitchen, complete with a huge walk-in fireplace, now serves as a cozy little lounge/tavern and, out back, is an enclosed porch with still another dining room.

The porch bustles a bit each morning as guests gather for their Continental breakfast and no doubt talk about their duckling à l'orange, pepper steak, veal scallops, chocolate mousse or dacquoise of the night before. For those inngoers on diets, this is definitely not the place to consider for long-term stays: the food is too good. And the rooms, gracing an 1806 structure a couple football fields away, too comfortable. They are furnished in period pieces and boast over-size bathrooms. On the ground floor there is an inviting living room for lounging about or planning the next day's activities.

COVENTRY FORGE INN, Route 23, Coventryville, Pennsylvania; mailing address: RFD 2, Pottstown, Pennsylvania 19464. Telephone: (215) 469-6222. Accommodations: five rooms; private baths; telephones; no televisions. Rates: moderate, includes Continental breakfast. Children permitted. No pets. Cards: AE, MC, VISA. Open all year except Christmas through January.

Getting There: Follow State Road 100 five miles south from Pottstown to State Road 23; turn right (west) and go 1.4 miles to the inn.

NORTHEASTERN PENNSYLVANIA

Turn-of-the-Century Quaintness
THE MOUNTAIN HOUSE
Delaware Water Gap, Pennsylvania

There is a Victorian vacation hotel quaintness about this 1870 three-story-high mountain inn, painted the compulsory pale yellow with green trim, *the* holiday tones a century ago for most mountain accommodations north and south. The lobby looks like a museum display of something your grandmother or great-grandmother walked through and there is a marvelous old registration book that probably goes back to the 1870 origins. Everywhere is wicker and antiques and patterned rugs. The rooms are rather spartan, but well-maintained and contain cherry, mahogany and oak beds. Out front is a grand old porch filled with rockers for doing nothing in the most pleasant of manners, breathing in all that fresh mountain air; or for resting after a day of exploring the all-embracing countryside of the Poconos a few feet from the inn. The Delaware Water Gap National Recreation Park is as close as the Appalachian Trail, lapped by the waters of the Delaware and Lake Lenape.

And when you return to the inn, there is that porch, or the sitting room with television and a raft of books and magazines, a swimming pool for warm weather, and an old-timey, rather large dining room where the fare is basic and solid. Innkeepers Frank and Yolanda Brown make you feel right at home here.

THE MOUNTAIN HOUSE, Mountain Road, Delaware Water Gap, Pennsylvania 18327. Telephone: (717) 424-2254. Accommodations: 35 rooms, 10 with private baths; no telephones; television in sitting room only. Rates: inexpensive, includes Continental breakfast. Children permitted. No pets. Cards: AE, CB, DC, MC, VISA. Open all year.

The Mountain House

Getting There: Mountain Road is at the southern end of Main Street (State Road 611) which runs through the center of town, off Exit 53 of Interstate 80.

The Innkeepers' Innkeepers

PINE KNOB
Canadensis, Pennsylvania

June and Jim Balfie, emigres from the insurance world somewhere in New Jersey, brought this dream to life in 1976 and, judging from the reactions of their guests—so many of them repeaters—they have realized dreams for many others as well. They care for the comforts of their guests; they are generous with their time; they found a superb chef (who trained at nearby Overlook Inn, noted for its food); they oversee a happy, cheerful staff which combines pleasantness with professional concern.

There are a variety of accommodations at Pine Knob: a bungalow for a couple out back, perfect for honeymooners, a pair of cottages and rooms in the inn itself. Favorites of mine are Room 20 with twin brass beds, Room 21 with dormer windows, and Room 22 with a beautiful cherry bed with a carved headboard found by the Belfies in 1982. They continue to search for antiques and accent pieces to furnish their happy little domain, not to clutter it, for they have too great a sense of restraint, of order, to overwhelm their rambling mansion, built originally as a tannery in 1847 and converted to an inn during the 1880s.

There is the same kind of good taste exhibited by the back room, with homemade everything: fresh-baked breads; Delmonico steaks slathered with shallot butter showered with mushrooms; duckling in an orange sauce reposing on a bed of wild rice; scallops in cream sauce; shrimp sautéed with chunks of sweet pepper kissed with garlic and softened with sherry; fresh trout baked in a brilliant herb lemon-white wine mélange and served with crispy almonds swimming in butter.

To work off those calories, consider a swim in the Pine Knob pool, a round of tennis or two, some badminton, shuffleboard, a jog around the inn's fifteen acres or farther afield. Or simply retreat to the antique-sparkling living room with its Steinway grand in the corner, which is put to good use for evening sing-alongs.

Artists should bring their easels and paint kits at any time of the year. But those who want to combine all this beauty and stimulation, all the warmth of the innkeepers, with some sharpening of their craft should consider the special Fall Art Workshops organized by the Belfies. They are five-day affairs commencing the second week in September and running for five sessions to the first week of November.

PINE KNOB, Route 447, Canadensis, Pennsylania 18325. Telephone: (717) 595-2532. Accommodations: 27 rooms; 19 with private baths; no telephones; no televisions. Rates: inexpensive to moderate, includes full breakfast and dinner, modified American plan. Children permitted. No pets. Cards: MC, VISA. Closed in December.

Getting There: Take the East Stroudsburg exit of Interstate 80 and follow State Road 447 fifteen miles to the inn, which is 1/2 mile south of the village of Canadensis.

Not to Be Overlooked

OVERLOOK INN
Canadensis, Pennsylvania

The Overlook Inn is a mini-resort surrounded by fifteen acres, laced with hiking and skiing trails laid out by innkeepers Lolly and Bob Tupper. They also installed the boccie, badminton and shuffleboard courts, and oversee the large pool. Close by are tennis courts and golf courses and the higher elevations of the Poconos for the slalom set.

But this is definitely not a resort in its accommodations, in its cozy Tupper's Tavern, in its rooms which are appointed with select antiques, an occasional quilt or two. There is no resort modernity, no glitz or phony glamour, no misfired attempts to be country inn cute and charming. But there is a dress code: jackets for the men at dinner, appropriate dress for the ladies, no swim suits in the public rooms.

That bit of formality adds to the atmosphere: the dining room is too special, the food too good to insult it with sloppiness. At breakfast the dress is, of course, less formal and when I was last at the Overlook there was a variety of clothing on those gearing up for a day of sports or exploring.

Breakfast began with fresh-squeezed orange juice, followed by superlative homemade sausage, buttermilk pancakes, raisin bran muffins, a Swiss cheese-mushroom omelet. Who needed lunch after that back-to-the-farm stocker? By dinner I was, however, famished and

65

did justice to the menu, a rather ambitious one. The dining room is open to the public for dinner although dinner as well as breakfast is included in the room tariff. The clams casino and oysters Rockefeller are commendable, the duck pâté velvety smooth, and the Pocono Mountain brook trout—farm-raised—and a filet of beef are superb. Also included amont the seventeen entrées are a brace of quail with wild rice, rabbit, lobster Thermidor, veal Oscar and Chateaubriand bouquetière. The desserts are nothing short of sensational, changed-daily delights, but count yourself fortunate if your stay coincides with the back room's production of a cheese cake with a raspberry brandy salute or the chocolate layer cake.

THE OVERLOOK INN, Dutch Mill Road, Canadensis, Pennsylvania 18325. Telephone: (717) 595-7519. Accommodations: 21 rooms; private baths; 12 rooms in main building, six in adjoining lodge, three in Carriage House; no telephones; no televisions. Rates: expensive, modified American plan—breakfast and dinner included with slight surcharges for certain menu items at dinner. Children under 12 and pets not permitted. Cards: AE, MC, VISA. Open all year.

Getting There: Canadensis is on State Roads 390 and 447; follow 447 north a quarter mile to the inn sign at Dutch Hill; take that 1-1/2 miles up the hill to the inn.

PUMP HOUSE INN

Canadensis, Pennsylvania

Here is yet another inn which concentrates on its food so seriously that it ranks among the outstanding restaurants in the nation. It *is* the best food in the Poconos; but than what other innkeeper is serving toad in the hole and cockie-leekie soup one night and gumbo, crevettes etouffée and praline mousse on another, alternating with fritto misto, suppa di pesce and zabaglione, or svartbrodsoppa, fisk med kremsaus, babaghanouj, tabboulah and baklava?

Those are just a few of the menu items on special evenings at the inn. All that plus a regular menu which shines with Pump House specialties such as calves' liver and scallions sautéed in a white wine-cream sauce bristling with passion fruit; poached salmon tossed with sour cream and presented on a bed of spinach mousse; bay scallops mingled with white wine sharpened with lemon and lime; chicken breast sporting a lobster mousse stuffing covered with a Calvados cream sauce; and fillets of salmon and sole filled with crab mousse then christened with a watercress cream sauce.

The Drucquer family, which has operated this inn since 1965, obviously cares about food and is concerned about breaking the dining out blahs. Start an evening here at their delightful little stone wall lounge with its huge fireplace and array of nautical memorabilia, looking over the menu and excellent wine list, working up an appetite all the while. And then don't worry about driving elsewhere. Check into one of the comfortably furnished rooms which are so cozy for two, looking forward to a Continental breakfast in the library—perhaps thinking of hanging on an extra night or two or three to indulge yourself again in all that sensational sustenance.

PUMP HOUSE INN, Skytop Road (P.O. Box 430), Canadensis, Pennsylvania 18325. Telephone: (717) 595-7501. Accommodations: six rooms; private baths; no telephones; no televisions. Rates: moderate, includes Continental breakfast. Children welcome. No pets. Cards: AE, CB, DC, MC, VISA. Open all year except for two weeks over Christmas and the month of January.

Getting There: Skytop Road is State Road 390 and the inn is 1.5 miles north of Canadensis on that road.

STERLING INN
South Sterling, Pennsylvania

For half a century this quintessential Poconos family resort vacation headquarters has been welcoming guests. I'm sure there are many repeaters, perhaps returning after summer holidays to do some cross-country skiing or to skate on the lake, or to watch the flaming foliage in the fall or the blooming apple, mountain laurel and rhododendron blossoms in the spring.

Fishermen favor the Wallenpaupack Creek, which trickles through the property and is a tributary of the Wallenpaupack, Pennsylvania's largest lake; golfers like the nearby courses; the let's-do-nothing set likes to sit on the lawn in sun or shade and wait for the next meal. Dinner is served only from 6 to 7:30, which says something about the groups vacationing here. Also, there is no liquor served, and the last time I made my rounds, the only antiques I could find were some of the guests.

But there were numerous family groups enjoying the comforts of the inn and the solidity of the food—strictly American Plan, with three meals included in the price of the lodging. And the rooms in the inn are very spacious, decorated in a manner that falls somewhere between middle-America and 1940s suburbia, which I'm sure is a welcome, homey kind of atmosphere for the regulars here. There are also cottages positioned strategically throughout the well-tended grounds, and they too are appealing to family groups or to those couples who want to get away from it all.

STERLING INN, Route 191, South Sterling, Pennsylvania 18460. Telephone: (717) 476-3311. Accommodations: 60 rooms; private baths; no telephones; no televisions. Rates: moderate, American plan. Children welcome. No pets. Cards: MC, VISA. Open all year.

Getting There: From the State Road 507 exit from Interstate 84, follow 507 south through Greentown and Newfoundland to State Road 191; follow 191 four miles south to the inn.

SETTLER'S INN
Hawley, Pennsylvania

The engaging little flyer put out by this inn states, "We've taken unlocked memories of calico living, then starched and ironed them with the warmth and friendliness that the traveler and vacationer would hope to enjoy." Everywhere that one looks in this rambling, barn-size hostelry, one finds that starched, clean, immaculately maintained look It is found in the individually decorated guestrooms ("they feature the loving and comfortable restoration of early attic furniture," the flyer continues), in the fireplace-filled sitting and dining rooms, accented with early tools and even a pair of skis. With liberal doses of warmth and friendliness.

Settler's Inn is, in the words of the flyer, "for guests who want a time for strolling the body and mind." They could have added, and for those who want to feed their faces. For this inn boasts a double-barrel team which puts it all together: innkeeper Jeanne Genalinger and her husband, Grant, who serves as chef. At noontime that means he prepares freshly assembled salads, a full parade of sandwiches, including freshly breaded haddock on a hard roll oozing with Dijonnaise sauce, and a Good Burger followed by a Better Burger followed by a Best Burger, in the manner of the old Sears catalogue. In the evening hours, Grant gets a lot more ambitious with veal given the traditional Oscar blessing or baked with tomatoes and Swiss cheese; with steaks

and chops; duckling; and shrimp stuffed with a cracker-breadcrumb combination or subjected to the standard scampi routine. And with all these possibilities there is a cart wheeled past the tables laden with the freshly baked breads of the day.

During crisp winter and fall evenings, there is no cozier spot than the Tavern in the Settler's Inn. The giant-size fireplace blazes away and there is a cheese bar, compliments of the management, along with plenty of easy-going, informal opportunity to greet other guests, to learn about area attractions, the antique and flea markets, the fishing and hunting sites, the tennis courts and golf courses, and about Lake Wallenpaupack with its half-hundred miles of shoreline.

SETTLER'S INN, 4 Main Avenue, Hawley, Pennsylvania 18428. Telephone: (717) 226-2993. Accommodations: 17 rooms; private baths; no telephones; no televisions. Rates: inexpensive to moderate. Children welcome. No pets. Cards: AE, DC, MC, VISA. Open all year.

Getting There: The inn is on the main street of the town, U.S. 6.

A Five-Star Find
THE INN AT STARLIGHT LAKE
Starlight, Pennsylvania

This inn nestled in the Moosic Range of the Appalachians, 900 acres of mostly unspoiled countryside dotted with 140 lakes and laced with winding roads and trails issuing year-round invitations to the hiker and, the explorer. In winter there are some twenty miles of marked trails for cross country skiers; in fall, paths for the hunters and those who come to admire the annual shifting of nature's colors; and in spring and summer there are canoeing, sailing, tennis, fishing, biking, croquet and shuffleboard, along with the spring-fed glistening waters of Starlight Lake, ideal for swimmers of all ages and degrees of skill.

But no matter the season, no matter the activity, it is always a joy to return to the inn's lobby with its cheerful, casual atmosphere and welcoming fireplace, then to proceed to the dining room with its well-prepared solid fare, some with surprisingly Continental overtones and German accents. Jaegerschnitzel in a summer hotel?

The rooms in the main inn, a three-story structure with a spacious front porch, are simply but comfortably furnished and have been a

The Inn at Starlight Lake

vacation retreat for city dwellers since 1909. There are also cottages for family groups, including my favorite accommodation here, Cottage 3C, a honeymoon hideaway with its own fireplace.

THE INN AT STARLIGHT LAKE, Starlight, Pennsylvania 18461. Telephone: (717) 798-2519. Accommodations: 30 rooms; 20 with private baths; no telephones; no televisions. Rates: moderate to expensive, includes breakfast and dinner, modified American plan. Lunch available in the dining room or as picnic, full bar. Children permitted. Pets not permitted, but a kennel is nearby. Cards: MC, VISA. Open all year except for two weeks in April.

Getting There: From Hancock, drive south on State Road 191, turning right onto State Road 370, following the signs to the inn.

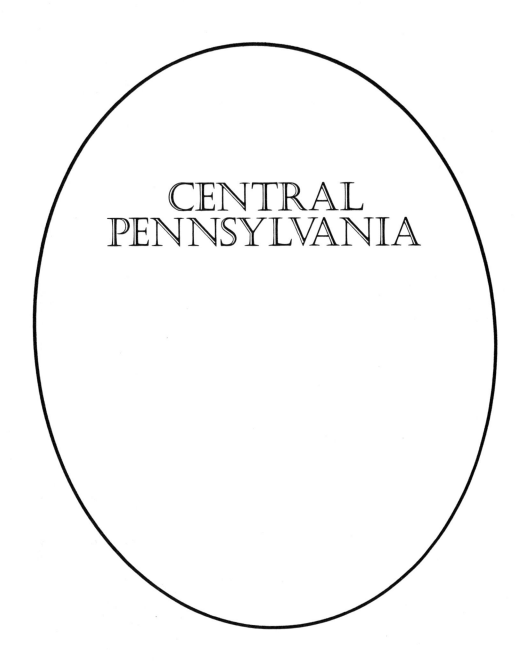

CENTRAL
PENNSYLVANIA

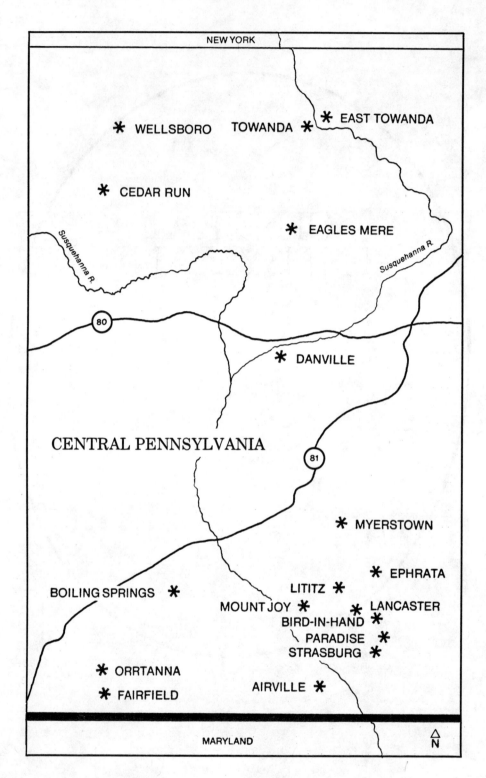

CENTRAL PENNSYLVANIA

NEW YORK

* WELLSBORO

TOWANDA * * EAST TOWANDA

* CEDAR RUN

* EAGLES MERE

Susquehanna R.

Susquehanna R.

80

* DANVILLE

81

* MYERSTOWN

* EPHRATA

LITITZ *

BOILING SPRINGS *

MOUNT JOY *

* LANCASTER

BIRD-IN-HAND *

PARADISE *

STRASBURG *

* ORRTANNA

* FAIRFIELD

AIRVILLE *

MARYLAND

N

NORTH CENTRAL
PENNSYLVANIA

Twentieth-Century Colonial
WILLIAMSTON INN
East Towanda, Pennsylvania

Just as surely as the Victorian Inn reflects its own turn-of-the-century era, so too does the Williamston reflect more modern times, with a touch of Colonial here and there. Opened in 1983, and sporting all the modern amenities plus a ramble of dining rooms which are usually packed noon and night, this is an up-to-date hostelry.

And its New Directions restaurant menu is up-to-date fun and games: with a chicken salad labeled Bird to the Wise (tuna is Whistle A Happy Tuna) and a breaded veal steak, Veal You Love Me? A quarter-pound burger rafted with "sauce from the mountain" is called The Breadless Horseman and the burger with steak fries and slaw is titled The All Time Chomp. Quiche and Tell covers that obvious category and Haley's Omelette is "A celestial event when we add our milkyway cheese to a galaxy of tomato, chives and eggs."

The menu alone is worth the effort to find this inn close to the banks of the Susquehanna and, I'm pleased to report, the food lives up to the advance billing, and the bar is a good one—as I learned one crisp fall day sipping on a Cider 'n Spice: warm apple cider spiked with ginger brandy, sugar and spices.

WILLIAMSTON INN, Route 6, East Towanda, Pennsylvania 18848. Telephone: (717) 265-8882. Accommodations: 16 rooms; private baths; telephones and televisions. Rates: moderate. Children welcome. No pets. Cards: AE, CB, DC, VISA. Open all year.

Getting There: The inn is across the Susquehanna River from Towanda, on the right side of the road past the curve after the bridge.

Victorian Victorious

VICTORIAN INN
Towanda, Pennsylvania

Barb Mower runs this immaculately maintained three-story, peaked-roof Victorian gem, complete with wraparound porches, carefully manicured gardens and a great sense of space. Located on the town's main street, which is lined with giant trees shading other magnificent mansions, this 1897 home has been a guest house for well over half a century. My favorite room here is number 1 with that wonderful four-poster bed, but all of the rooms have something to appeal to the visitor or the businessman (Sylvania, Du Pont and Masonite constitute the main industries in the area).

And the town has a time-stood-still appeal about it: walking past those Victorian echoes, admiring the courthouse with that splendid monument to the Civil War dead, thinking back to the days when the young Stephen Foster attended Towanda Academy in the 1840s. Maybe it was here where he first saw those Conestoga wagons heading west with the pioneers, where he first thought up some of the words to that song they took with them to new homes—"Oh Susanna!"

VICTORIAN INN, 118 York Avenue, Towanda, Pennsylvania 18848. Telephone: (717) 265-6972. Accommodations: 10 rooms; 6 with private baths; telephones; televisions. Rates: moderate, includes complimentary coffee. Children under 12 and pets not permitted. Open all year.

Getting There: The inn is on the main street of the town.

Mere is More

EAGLES MERE INN
Eagles Mere, Pennsylvania

A mere is an archaic term for a small lake or pool and I suppose at one time in the century-long history of this three-story with its splendid front porch, gables and fireplaces, there were eagles circling the lake. Maybe they are still winging about today: I did not see any when I made my reconaissance, breathing in the cool, clean air at three thousand feet, thinking that I could see into infinity from the peaks of what they term the Endless Mountains in the Alleghenies.

Perhaps the Fiocchis, Lou and Joan, who took over the inn back in 1983, have been keeping track of their feathered friends in addition to all their other responsibilities: supervising the kitchen serving breakfast and dinner to the public as well as inn guests, maintaining the putting green and the grounds, planting the annuals every spring, and directing guests to the nearby Sullivan County Historical Museum, World's End State Park, and of course Eagles Mere Lake.

Their redecorating chores have been completed, they greatly expanded the wine list, made their menus more diversified and in general did a sprucing-up. But they did not gussie it up; the inn is still an unspoiled escape in a largely unspoiled part of the country. There is a quartet of covered bridges in the Endless Mountains, all kinds of hunting and fishing possibilities—a Bow Hunters Festival is held each September, tennis and golf at the nearby Country Club (inn guests are given full privileges), hiking and horseback riding, numerous ski trails, and a long toboggan run where the sleds rush down the hill onto Eagles Mere Lake at speeds up to fifty miles an hour.

EAGLES MERE INN, P.O. Box 356, Eagles Mere, Pennsylvania 17731. Telephone: (717) 525-3273. Accommodations: 30 rooms;

private baths; no telephones or televisions. Rates: moderate, includes breakfast and dinner during spring, summer and fall. Children welcome. No pets. Cards: AE, MC, VISA. Open daily May 1–November 1; weekends only during other months.

Getting There: Take exit 34 on Interstate 80, following State Road 42 north 33 miles to the town and the inn.

Wynken, Blynken and Nod
PENN WELLS HOTEL
Wellsboro, Pennsylvania

This hostelry is as neat and fussily maintained as the Main Street it sits on; but then this entire town has the appearance of having been thoroughly cleaned yesterday. Maple trees line the thoroughfares; there is a village green across from the Tioga County Court House complete with a Union trooper high atop a pedestal and a fountain with a wee boat holding Eugene Field's Wynken, Blynken and Nod. Having attended, in my youth, Eugene Field Elementary School—named for the children's poet-journalist-blithe spirit who put those waifs in the boat—this memorial was a pleasant surprise.

But then so was everything else in this sleepy little settlement with a country inn of a hotel owned and operated by the community—and built by that community too. Rooms are functional but filled with pretty fabrics and sturdy furniture; there is a large American flag in the lobby; the dining room features good luncheon salads; and at night a well-stocked salad and appetizer bar, along with entrées of crisp duckling, filet mignon, lobster tail and Icelandic haddock.

If that is not to your liking, go around the corner to the vintage diner with its "Draw one!" "Hold the mustard!" atmosphere. Or take a picnic ten miles out to the Leonard Harrison State Park and Pennsylvania's very own Grand Canyon, forty miles of four-season activity and sightseeing. Springtime rafting rocks along the fifty-mile, thousand-foot gorge of Pine Creek, and during hunting season, there is no greater challenge to be met than trying to find the elusive wild turkey. The county stocks some hundred miles of streams with trout and each June there is the Pennsylvania Laurel Festival. This is when bands and strutting majorettes parade the town's streets—gaslit boulevards recalling the earlier years of a city founded in 1806 and settled

Penn Wells Hotel

primarily by pioneers who poured across the wilderness from New England. For a map to the many primitive roads that wind in and out of the Grand Canyon, check with the Tioga Association of Recreation and Tourism at the Courthouse Annex in Wellsboro. Or talk with one of the friendly natives, the person behind the desk at the inn.

PENN WELLS HOTEL, 62 Main Street, Wellsboro, Pennsylvania 16901. Telephone: (717) 724-2111. Accommodations: 89 rooms; 75 private baths; telephones; televisions. Rates: inexpensive. Full bar and meal service. Children and pets permitted. Cards: AE, DC, MC, VISA. Open all year.

Getting There: Wellsboro is 45 miles from Elmira, New York and 55 miles from Williamsport, Pennsylvania at the intersection of U.S. 6 and State Road 287; the hotel is in the center of town.

Rustic Retreat
CEDAR RUN INN
Cedar Run, Pennsylvania

In the heart of Pine Creek Gorge high in the mountains of North Central Pennsylvania, where there are more animals than people and more trails than roads, this wonderfully rustic inn serves as an ideal escape from the smog and congestion of the city. Or as a happily run base camp for sportsmen who find their way here year after year to fish and hunt during the season. Or to glide their canoes along sparkling streams, do a bit of white-water rafting, or in winter swish along snowy trails, on skis or with snowmobile.

Guest rooms here are not elaborate—that would be an insult to the countryside—but they are comfortable, and there is plenty of public space, including a front porch lined with rockers, for telling tall tales about the one that got away.

The real surprise is the quality of the food. One expects hearty fare in these parts, and chef Randy Lounsbury, who with wife Peggy Myers runs the place, does provide generous portions. But he also displays considerable talent: sautéing sole with shrimp and kiwi then finishing with lemon butter; filling pork loin with ground apples and hazelnuts and finishing that with an apple/brandy sauce; poaching scallops with green grapes and mushrooms aggrandized by a lobster sauce; sautéing rainbow trout with lump crabmeat, sliced cucumbers and segments of lime. And for desserts there is a marvelously lemony cheese pie, a praline parfait every bit as good as those featured at Commander's Palace in New Orleans, and smoked gouda produced at the nearby Caleb's Cheese House. With this much good food, one has to get out and hunt, fish, hike or ski all day.

CEDAR RUN INN, Cedar Run, Pennsylvania 17727. Telephone: (717) 353-6241. Accommodations: 13 rooms: four private baths; no telephones; no televisions. Rates: moderate. Children welcome. No pets. No cards. Open Wednesdays through Sundays, April through December; weekends only February –March; closed the month of January.

Getting There: Lake State Road 287 twelve miles south to Morris; turn right (west) on State Road 414 and follow it 9 miles through Blackwell to Cedar Run where there is a sign for the inn.

Recuperate and Recover
PINE BARN INN
Danville, Pennsylvania

The Pine Barn Inn is across the road from the Geisinger Medical Center, an important back-up emergency facility and trauma center in this central area of Pennsylvania, with Life Flight helicopter transport, five intensive care units and hundreds of specially trained technicians and doctors. This comfortable spread of rooms, furnished in Colonial fashion, provides a convenient headquarters for those visiting someone at the Center or those who merely want to escape into the quiet of the Pennsylvania countryside. Or for those who want to explore the area: the streams of Columbia County—which attract thousands of anglers every year—are a fishing paradise. In fact, it is rumoured in town that the angler has to hide behind the trees to bait his hook!

There is also hunting in season, hiking at any time of the year, old stone churches and farmhouses to explore, a wealth of farms and orchards, and the nearby Knoebels Grove amusement park with some thirty rides for the kids, giant water slides and roller skating. Columbia and Montour Counties declare they constitute the Covered Bridge Capital of the country, and with twenty-five of them and an Annual

Covered Bridge Festival each October they have good reason to make such a claim.

The last week in September features another annual event, the Bloomsburg Agricultural Fair, a 125-year-old tradition spread over close to two hundred acres with all kinds of stock, home crafts and industrial arts on display, plus a race track for horses and autos and a center stage for big-name entertainers.

At the base camp of the Pine Barn Inn, given that name for its core structure built in the 1870s and beautifully restored in 1967, is an excellent restaurant. Rambling through the old barn, with its fieldstone foundation walls, exposed beams and rugged Old Country furnishings, the dining room is surely the class act of this section of central Pennsylvania. The back room produces a classic Continental menu, everything from creamy scallops to crisp duckling, from crabmeat imperial splashed with sherry, to all kinds of seafood and superior veal creations. There is also a well-stocked relish and salad bar.

Inn guestrooms are more motel modern in appearance on the outside but innkeepers Barbara and Martin Walzer have furnished them with considerable taste, reflecting the rustic atmosphere of this section of the state.

PINE BARN INN, Danville, Pennsylvania 17821. Telephone: (717) 275-2071. Accommodations: 45 rooms; private baths; telephones and televisions. Rates: inexpensive. Full bar and restaurant. Children welcome. Pets permitted in some rooms but inquire. Cards: AE, MC, VISA. Open all year.

Getting There: Take Exit 33 of Interstate 80 and drive south on State Route 54 three miles, turning left at the first traffic light at the sign for the Geisinger Medical Center, which is across the road from the inn.

SOUTH CENTRAL
PENNSYLVANIA

Total Immersion
TULPEHOCKEN MANOR INN AND PLANTATION
Myerstown, Pennsylvania

The Lebanon Valley is rich in history and in natural beauty, and this 150-acre plantation provides the perfect base camp for understanding the past and exploring that beauty. As well as appreciating the present, for this plantation with its cluster of old stone structures is a working farm. And its buildings are museums, open to the public daily from 11 a.m. to 5 p.m. for guided tours. They include the 1769 Michael Ley Mansion—George Washington slept there—with fourteen museum-quality rooms for overnight guests, the 1750 Christopher Ley Big Spring House and the Michael Spangler Little Spring House of the same vintage, and the 1886 Cyrus Sherk House.

The houses are ideal for families and for those who want to leave the grounds when the public arrives. There is a great deal to see in this valley, including the production plants where all that famous Lebanon bologna is made. At nearby Cornwall, at the intersection of Rexmont Road and Miner's Village Road, is the Cornwall Furnace Museum, a proudly preserved property dating from 1742, next to one of the largest man-made, open-pit mines in the world: until 1973 it was the richest and most productive ore mass in North America. At Cornwall, arms and ammunition were made for Washington's Colonial army; the general visited the furnace with Lafayette when encamped at Valley Forge.

Cornwall Furnace owner Peter Grubb expanded his holdings after the Revolution, purchasing land to the south and building a magnificent sandstone mansion, which was greatly expanded a century later into a masterpiece of Victorian exaggeration. It now serves as the main building of the Mount Hope Winery where guided tours are regularly given, ending in the billiard room with a tasting of Pennsylvania wines.

83

Southeast of Myerstown and the Tulpehocken Inn (the name comes from the Indian term for the valley) is Historic Schaefferstown, where descendents of the original settlers hold weekend seminars and give demonstrations, attracting scholars and tourists eager to learn more about life in the eighteenth century. The site is a ninety-acre farm, open to visitors June though September. Each June there is a Cherry Festival and a Folklore Festival and there is a Harvest and Horseplowing Festival in September. The nation's oldest distillery, built in 1753, is two miles south of Schaefferstown and is open to the public.

East of the inn is Zeller's Fort, a National Historic Site and a fine example of early Rhine Basin architecture, built originally from logs but then rebuilt of limestone in 1745.

West of the inn, close to the town of Lebanon, is the oldest existing man-made tunnel in the nation—a 729-foot engineering marvel of its time. Farther west is the seventy-six-acre Hersheypark which surrounds Chocolate Town, U.S.A. There is a free display complex and a fine gift center, twenty-three acres of beautifully tended gardens (open April through October) and the superb Hershey Museum of American Life, along with a hotel oddly designed in the Spanish style but boasting an excellent dining room.

There is no food service at the Tulpehocken, so the Hershey should be kept in mind. That or some of those bologna makers.

TULPEHOCKEN MANOR INN AND PLANTATION, 650 West Lincoln Avenue, Myerstown, Pennsylvania 17067. Telephone: (717) 866-4926. Accommodations: 14 rooms in the Ley Mansion; shared baths; the three other houses with private baths are available for longer-term rental, the Ley House with a minimum one week require-

84

ment, the Sherk House minimum three nights and the Spangler House for a week, month or longer. No telephones or televisions. Rates: moderate to expensive. Children permitted. No pets. No cards. Open all year.

Getting There: The inn is on U.S. 422 five miles east of Lebanon.

A Model Restoration

SMITHTON INN

Ephrata, Pennsylvania

This inn first opened its doors in June 1763. Henry Miller and his wife, Susana, were the innkeepers. They were also members of the Ephrata Cloister, that unique German Protestant religious movement founded forty years earlier by a charismatic pietistic mystic named Conrad Beissel. The Millers were members of the householders order; the two other orders were monastic, celibate, severely spartan, sleeping on board benches and using wooden pillows.

Together the three orders established one of the earliest religious communities in the country and they were excellent farmers and craftsmen—printing books, making paper and building a chapel, dormitories and work rooms in the medieval manner that they remembered from their homes in the Rhineland. They printed the largest book of Colonial times, the 1,200-page *Martyrs Mirror* for the Mennonites and their press, the "new" one brought to their community in 1804, is still in use today.

Visitors to the Ephrata Cloister (open every day but Monday) can see the press plus the carefully restored buildings now maintained by the State Historical and Museum Commission; from late June to early September on Saturday evenings and on certain Sundays, there is *Vorspiel,* a musical drama presenting life at the Cloister.

When making plans to attend and visit the community, also make plans to stay at the Smithton Inn. A model of model restorations, it is a beautifully revitalized, solid stone structure with fireplaces, library and living room handsomely furnished with great taste. The blue room is a real beauty, with gray-blue trim, a blue-draped four-poster covered with a lovely quilt and a hooked rug on the highly polished floor.

The suites are also special here: they have their own entrances and porch, along with a kitchenette and living room with fireplace, double canopy bed and cupboard bed. And outside, the gardens with the all-important fruit trees have been restored with as much care and concern for authenticity as the rest of the building. The gazebo overlooking all this manicured lushness is ideal for breakfast.

SMITHTON INN, 900 West Main St. and Academy Drive, Ephrata, Pennsylvania 17522. Telephone: (717) 733-6094. Accommodations: atwo rooms and two suites; private baths; no telephones; television in room. Rates: moderate to expensive. Children welcome. No pets. Cards: AE, MC, VISA. Open all year.

Getting There: The inn is 3/10 mile from the Ephrata Cloister, at the traffic light on the corner of Main Street and Academy Drive.

HISTORIC 1725 WITMER'S TAVERN
Lancaster, Pennsylvania

At one time there were some sixty-two inns and taverns along the nation's first turnpike, the one which ran between Philadelphia and Lancaster—or Hickorytown as it was then called—in the pre-Revolutionary era. Today only Witmer's survives. And it survives in great style and authenticity, a tribute to the past, to those pioneers in their Conestoga wagons who rolled along the Old Philadelphia Pike to the oldest inland town in America at that time, and then on to the unknown, beyond the Susquehanna River.

There were a Amish farmers in those early days, and there are still Amish farmers: their fields surround the town and their plain, black carriages roll past this inn just as they have for centuries. Information on the Amish and other essential data for use in exploring the countryside and for learning more about Pennsylvania Dutch country and the nearby attractions is available at the Mennonite Information Center and the Pennsylvania Dutch Visitors Center, a short walk from the inn.

Seven of the inn rooms have been carefully restored to reflect their simple pioneer past. The paint colors follow those originally brushed on walls: blue in the Jefferson suite, pumpkin in the suite named for French General Lafayette which has an eighteenth-century cannonball rope bed. An Acorn rope bed is in another room and five of the rooms have working fireplaces (there is an extra charge for the firewood). One of the rooms, the one with a fine Colonial corner cupboard, is the rallying point for inn guests: to have their complimentary coffee and pastries in the mornings, to gather again at night to exchange stories and sayings about the Pennsylvania Dutch, to get first-hand reports on the restaurants. There are books and magazines, cards and games and sheets of information detailing the history of this historic hostelry which has been on the National Register of Historic Places since 1978.

HISTORIC 1725 WITMER'S TAVERN, 2014 Old Philadelphia Pike, Lancaster, Pennsylvania 17602. Telephone: (717) 299-5305. Accommodations: five rooms with shared baths; no telephones or televisions. Rates: inexpensive to moderate, includes Continental breakfast. Children welcome. No pets. No cards. Open all year.

Getting There: Take U.S. East Bypass from Lancaster to exit for State Road 340; the inn is a few hundred yards from the exit on 340, on the right side.

GREYSTONE MOTOR LODGE
Bird-In-Hand, Pennsylvania

More inn than lodge, more Victorian mansion than motor hotel, its origins go back to the middle of the nineteenth century when a farm house was built on a prominence of land overlooking the Old Philadelphia Turnpike. In 1883 a three-story stone and brick house in the French Victorian style was built as stunning evidence of the prosperity of its owner, and a century later the old barn was converted to carriage house.

The present-day owners, Jim and Phyllis Reed, honor the history and the heritage, tending their two acres with liberal doses of tender lovin' care, preserving all that beveled glass, the plaster casts on the walls and medallions on the ceilings, the original woodwork, the old bath fixtures, and the antique furnishings. And they also keep a storehouse of brochures on the many area attractions and can update information on the restaurants. Close by is the Bird-In-Hand Farmers' Market, midway between Smoketown and Intercourse, the Good 'N Plenty Restaurant, the world's shortest covered bridge and The Old Village Store. At the store you can learn about the name of this little village: it came from the sign that swung outside an inn dating from Colonial times: the sign pictured a painting of a bird grasped by a hand.

GREYSTONE MOTOR LODGE, 2658 Old Philadelphia Pike (State Road 340), Bird-In-Hand, Pennsylvania 17505. Telephone: (717) 393-4233. Accommodations: 12 rooms; private baths; two with kitchenettes; televisions; no telephones. Rates: inexpensive, includes coffee and doughnuts in the morning. Children welcome. No pets. Cards: AE, MC, VISA. Closed from November 15 to March 1.

Getting There: The inn is on the south side of State Road 340 one block west of the railroad overpass in Bird-In-Hand.

Greystone Motor Lodge

MAPLE LANE FARM GUEST HOUSE
Paradise, Pennsylvania

It is hard for me to write a country inns book without putting in some kind of back-to-the-farm experiences, something to take the kids to, to escape completely from the city—and even from charming, sometimes overdone, or too-cute country inns. Maple Lane Farm is precisely that kind of place. Buried in the heart of Amish country, it is a working farm, a 250-acre expanse with some 180 head of cattle, about half of them dairy cows.

If you get up with the cows, you can watch the milking—the farmers here don't mind your watching any part or parcel of their daily routines. Then walk around the rolling meadows and climb to hilltops for views across the woods and the tidily kept farms which sometimes resemble the kind of toy village found around model railroad sets. There are two acres of lawn in front of the farmhouse and a quiet little stream winding its way through the property. The original farmstead, an 1875 fieldstone structure built by an immigrant from Germany, is across from the larger building where the accommodations are and where innkeepers Marion and Edwin Rohrer live.

Marion is responsible for those hand-made quilts in each of the guest rooms as well as for the needlepoint on the chairs. In the living room and each of the individual rooms, there are antique pieces representing a conglomerate rather than coordinated approach to collecting, but everywhere there is the sense of country simplicity, of rural honesty.

MAPLE LANE FARM GUEST HOUSE, 505 Paradise Lane, Paradise, Pennsylvania 17562. Telephone: (717) 687-7479. Accommodations: four rooms; two with private baths; no telephones; no televisions. Rates: inexpensive. Children permitted. No pets. No cards. Open all year.

Getting There: 1.5 miles from Strasburg on State Road 896, turn onto Paradise Lane.

HISTORIC STRASBURG INN
Strasburg, Pennsylvania

The "historic" part only goes back to the 1970s, but they claim a longer heritage—all the way back to 1793. That is the year the Washington House accommodated its first visitors in the heart of town, the main square. It was an inn until 1921 and is now reborn in this replica a mile north forming the core of a spacious, 58-acre complex of comfortably furnished rooms, complete with all the modern amenities, along with rockers, print wallpaper and comfortable beds—all executed in a modern Colonial, Williamsburg kind of style.

The Washington House, with the several dining rooms named after the owners of the ancient hostelry, Asbury, Hoffman, Musselman, Whitehill (also Colonial with a serving staff straight out of a Martha Washington tea party), is the site of special seasonal celebrations. Christmas with the ceremonial burning of the yule log, trimming of the tree, singing of carols, and feasting, is an especially entertaining time.

Among the regular specialties of the inn's kitchen are prime rib with Yorkshire pudding; crispy duckling glazed with fresh raspberry sauce; mixed grill and saltimbocca; a pork chop stuffed with apples, prunes, almonds and bread covered with rich pan gravy; lump crabmeat seasoned sensationally and then baked; trout dredged in spiced cornmeal-pecan crumbs; and something called Jamestown Pye, a crab-shrimp mélange suspended with bits of other seafood in a rich cream sauce before being baked en croûte.

All the breads, rolls and pastries are baked on the premises. On Friday nights there are seafood buffets and on Sundays a bountiful brunch with sixty-plus selections to choose from. There is also an adjacent gift shop with local handicrafts for sale, a large lobby with fireplace, bike and hiking paths, and ample information for exploring the Pennsylvania Dutch town, Strasburg.

A mile distant is the Amish Village, with guided tours of an old Amish farmhouse, a one-room school, farm animals and an operating smokehouse. Here also is the Mill Bridge Village with a long covered bridge, carriage rides, a bakery putting out such local specialties as shoo-fly pie and funnel cakes. East of the inn is the Strasburg Railroad with daily rides (May through October) through the scenic Lancaster County landscape, a museum of toy trains, the Choo-Choo Barn with a fantastic model train display, and the Red Caboose Lodge, a gathering of twenty cabooses, each with a different line's logo brightly painted on the sides. The old railroad cars are now a motel and the Victorian dining coaches make up the dining rooms. The staff is garbed in suitable outfits and the manager, when I toured these bedrooms for railroad buffs, smiled from under his conductor's cap and said, "We're the only hotel in existence where we guarantee you get out of bed on the right track."

The engines of course are all steam powered: inventor Robert Fulton was born close by—in 1765 in the village of Little Britain, renamed Fulton some years later.

HISTORIC STRASBURG INN, Route 896, Strasburg (Lancaster County), Pennsylvania 17579.Telephone: (717) 687-7691. Accommodations: 103 rooms, suites and second-floor Dutchland View rooms with covered front balconies, private baths; telephones; televisions; AM/FM radio. Rates: moderate to expensive. Full bar and meal service. Children welcome. Pets: $25 deposit. Cards: AE, DC, MC, VISA.

Getting There: The inn is a mile north of Strasburg on State Road 896.

Marvelous Metamorphosis
STRASBURG VILLAGE INN
Strasburg, Pennsylvania

This classic country inn started that way—in the post-revolutionary days as brave pioneers were making their way to the wilds of the west. Known then as Crawford's Tavern, the first town council, elected after the War of 1812, met here. Years later, it housed the local post office and then a country store, also a community meeting place. Today the country store, the Strasburg Country Store & Creamery, is next door. It is a wonderful place for ice cream and snacks and for buying locally produced handicrafts and souvenirs.

The inn was reborn in May 1984, wonderfully transformed into something of beauty and elegance, with eleven handsomely furnished rooms—furnished with antiques of course—and a second floor sitting room for guests to gather and exchange Pennsylvania Dutch stories or do a bit of reading. Downstairs, the front porch is a perfect staging area for watching all the action on this strip of historic district, a two-mile

spread that was one of the first to be registered in the country, or to sit a spell before heading to the Washington House for dinner at the Historic Strasburg Inn.

STRASBURG VILLAGE INN, Centre Square, 1 West Main Street, Strasburg, Pennsylvania 17579. Telephone: (717) 687-0900. Accommodations: 11 rooms including four suites, two with jacuzzi and skylight, one with private porch; private baths; no telephones or televisions. Rates: moderate to expensive, includes Continental breakfast. Children permitted. No pets. Cards: AE, VISA. Open all year.

Getting There: The inn is in the center of Strasburg's Historic District, in the main square on the main street.

Moravian Marvels
GENERAL SUTTER INN
Lititz, Pennsylvania

Why name an inn in Pennsylvania Dutch Country after California's premier pioneer? Why give the name of the German-born Swiss, at whose mill gold was first discovered, to an old and honorable hostelry which the Moravian church established in 1764?

The answers are simple. After suffering severe financial losses at his fort in Sacramento, losing thousands of acres in the process, Sutter and his family moved east, escaping the greed, the frenzy and the insanity of the West during the Gold Rush. Few places on earth could have been as opposite in philosophy and peacefulness as Lititz, named by the Moravians who settled here in the 1740s, creating their own "Land Gemeine," named for a Bohemian town which sheltered persecuted Moravians in 1456.

In 1764 they built an inn, Zum Anker (Sign of the Anchor), noted from its earliest days as a place for good food—and for no frivolity. Dancing was not allowed, nor was cursing, gossip or bawdy songs. In 1803 it was rebuilt and forty-five years later, bricks were laid, additions made, and it took the form it has today.

When General Sutter arrived, it was known as the Springs Hotel, and he liked it and the area so much that after spending a summer there he had a home built directly across the street. It was the first in town to have hot and cold running water, and in addition, it had a superb wine cellar—Sutter was one of the first to promote California wines!

The home, in an admirable state of repair, still stands, as do many of the other homes flanking Main Street which were erected by the early settlers. There are more than a dozen, including the Joseph Sturgis Home built in 1782 by the town's potter. It was declared by Sutter to be the most beautiful in town, and it has been kept in its time capsule almost totally intact. At 221 Main Street is the 1784 Peter Kreider House, where the first commercially produced pretzels originated. At 145 Main Street is the Schropp House from 1793: Schropp was a nailsmith, schoolteacher and church organist. The Johannes Mueller House from 1792 was built by the community dyer and his home now serves as the town museum and headquarters of the Lititz Historical Foundation, which has furnished it with authentic pieces and an interesting collection of early Moravian artifacts.

Across the street is Moravian Church Square with its Brethren's House from 1759—it served as hospital during the American Revolution—and Linden Hall, one of the two oldest girls' schools in the country. Behind the church is God's Acre, the Moravian Cemetery where, by special dispensation of the Moravian Church, Lutheran Sutter is buried along with his wife, Anna Duebeld. Sutter died alone, in a

94

Washington D.C. hotel room—despondent in his most recent lack of success petitioning Congress for redress of his many grievances and compensation for his losses.

Across the street from the inn which honors Sutter is Lititz Springs Park (the mineral springs once attracted many, including Sutter, who hoped to cure rheumatism) where on Sunday evenings at 7 from July through September there are evening vespers.

This is a most appropriate practice in this village where the buggies of the Simple Folk, the Amish, are always very much in evidence. Everywhere in town are signs of their presence. But the inn is as much Victorian in its decor as it is reflective of the period when the Moravians built it. Louis XIV sofas in floral brocade, elaborately carved marble top coffee table, brass and crystal parlor lamps and a dining room called Gaslight Pub with cranberry walls bespeak a more elaborate approach to life than that found in the architecture and design of all the Moravian leftovers on Main Street.

But the antique-filled rooms are comfortable and extremely well-maintained, the coffee shop for breakfast and lunch is a breezy delight and I like the tree-shaded brick patio out front where during summer months, one can watch the passing parade.

GENERAL SUTTER INN, 14 East Main Street, On the Square, Lititz, Pennsylvania 17543. Telephone: (717) 626-2115. Accommodations: 11 rooms; private baths; telephones; televisions. Rates: inexpensive. Full bar and meal service. Children welcome. Inquire about pets. Cards: AE, MC, VISA. Open all year.

Getting There: Lititz is seven miles north of Lancaster on State Road 501 and the inn is on the square and is impossible to miss.

From Restaurateur to Innkeeper

CAMERON ESTATE INN
Mount Joy, Pennsylvania

Another one of the inns in this book listed on the National Register of Historic Places, painstakingly restored in the 1980s by the same Groff clan who worked similar miracles on a 1756 farm house four miles away. Now known as Groff's Farm Restaurant, it features fantastically fine American fare fresh from the fields and farms: specialties include chicken Stoltzfus which spells tender chunks of roast chicken suspended in a rich cream sauce and dolloped over the flakiest of freshly baked pastry shells.

Their newest venture also has a restaurant, with a super Sunday champagne brunch with terrific French toast in Grand Marnier-spiked sauce and superb crêpes stuffed with chicken or seafood. Dinner headliners include fresh rainbow trout coated with crushed pecans and corn flour, sautéed in lemon butter and kissed with a splendid white wine sauce; steak Diane; sirloin béarnaise; duckling in a mandarin orange sauce; and a chicken named for the most famous owner of the estate, Simon Cameron: it is wrapped around hickory-smoked ham, sautéed in garlic butter and served with white asparagus and a wine-cheese sauce.

Some might argue a crow should have been substituted for the chicken, so questionable were some of the statements and actions of President Lincoln's first Secretary of War. Cameron, four times senator and Ambassador to Russia (where he did gain the Czar's support of the Union), was the first of the powerful state "bosses" and he was a vocal and vigorous supporter of the political patronage system.

He bought the estate in 1872. Located next door to the 1730 Donegal Church and close to where Cameron was born, the original home on the property was built in 1805 by Dr. John Watson, great-grandfather of President William McKinley, and it was one of the largest homes on the Susquehanna frontier. In 1895 Cameron's son, James, also a U.S. Senator and former Secretary of War in U.S. Grant's cabinet, enlarged the home considerably, winding up with a total of twenty-five rooms.

For a time it was used as conference center by Elizabethtown College and it still has a conference center, as integral attraction of the inn. Today it is strictly country inn with a happy surplus of class. Surrounded by fifteen acres of quiet, and boasting rooms that are

Cameron Estate Inn

individually decorated, some with king-size canopy beds, others with four-posters, six with working fireplaces (firewood is extra), all with considerable charm, this inn is a restful, spacious retreat for all seasons.

THE CAMERON ESTATE INN, R.D. #1 (Box 305), Mount Joy, Pennsylvania 17552. Telephone: (717) 653-1773. Accommodations: 18 rooms; two share baths, others private; telephones; television in sitting room. Rates: expensive, includes Continental breakfast. Children under 12 and pets not permitted. Cards: AE, MC, VISA. Open all year.

Getting There: The inn is 3 miles from Mount Joy; from Lancaster on Donegal Springs Road which runs between Mount Joy and the Susquehanna River.

Total Escape
THE SPRING HOUSE
Airville, Pennsylvania

Of all the inns I have visited in this country and abroad, The Spring House is one of my favorites, earning this position because of its isolated location, its surrounding countryside, its solid, old-fashioned comforts and perhaps above all, because of its innkeeper—Ray Constance Hearne, a gentle, witty, energetic Quaker lady of many interests and talents. She has a pair of cats for companions, and a spaniel called Hadrian, the resident tour guide who will lead guests along the abandoned rail bed of the Ma and Pa Railroad (as the locals labeled the Maryland and Pennsylvania line).

Nearby Muddy Creek is one of the state's loveliest ribbons of water—despite the name—filled with fish and scenic shores. Along the Susquehanna is the Mason-Dixon trail, and nearby fields and farms are filled with the bounty of the fertile land. Inn guests can pick strawberries in the spring, then all kinds of berries (Ray has her own bushes, source for her splendid homemade jams and preserves dispensed each morning), cherries, apples and pears. Ray raises all her own herbs and local farmers provide the fresh milk and eggs which go into her breakfasts built around cakes and breads and preserves, fritatas and kugelhopfs, cooked on her wood-burning stove. Her pies and breads and sparkling cider have won blue ribbons at the local county fair and this farm-girl-turned-art-student (Antioch College)-turned innkeeper could no doubt run a top flight restaurant specializing in honest regional fare. She does do dinners on special occasions.

Innkeeper Hearne also organizes special theme weekends, offering lessons in breadbaking on that stove, vegetarian Indian cooking, and the use of herbs and culinary wreath-making; tours and tasting at three local wineries (including Allegro in nearby Brogue which won a gold medal at the Eastern Wine Competition for its 1980 cabernet sauvignon); stenciling; Christmas tree gathering and decorating; and special musical happenings—classical song, Welsh music in the Welsh settlement of Delta.

Guests at Spring House, whether or not assembled for one of these stimulating events, really live as their grandparents did. There is no heat in the second-floor bedrooms—but plenty of thick comforters, quilts and feather beds. And a fine display of stenciling, most of it done by friend and local artist Peggy Kurtz. One of the rooms has a Jenny Lind spool bed, another an 1820 blanket roll bed, another a sleeping porch for nighttime star-gazing. Smoking is not allowed in these rooms—or anywhere else in the house—which is crisply maintained with white-washed walls and an interesting collection of clay pots filled with wild flowers.

A walk in any direction from the Spring House is rewarding, but for those who want more purpose, there is the town of York with its county courthouse where the Continental Congress, chased from Philadelphia by the British, signed the all-important Articles of Confederation. A multi-media presentation explains the history. Then there is the 1741 Golden Plough Tavern, General Gates House and the Currier and Ives gallery with more than four hundred of their original lithographs. Airville has an interesting Indian Steps Museum with nearby bird sanctuary and hiking trail. On Mothers' Day, York has its annual street fair with all kinds of performing groups and craftsmen. In August there is a Gemutlicheit Festival with the Germans doing their oompah thing at the fairgrounds and the following month there is the Interstate Fair, the country's oldest, started in 1765 and now running a full nine days with numerous agricultural exhibits and big-name entertainment. There is also a Halloween parade, largest of any such event at any time of the year.

SPRING HOUSE, Muddy Creek Forks, York County, Airville, Pennsylvania 17302. Telephone: (717) 927-6906. Accommodations: four rooms upstairs sharing bath; one room on ground floor with private bath; public telephone; no televisions. Rates: moderate, includes full breakfast. Children permitted. No pets. Cards: MC, VISA. Open all year.

Getting There: In the center of Airville, southeast of York on State Road 74, take the road to Woodbine for 1.2 miles to a fork; take the road on the right, Frosty Hill, to the end of the road and turn left to the inn. But do not plan to find the inn in the dark; it is better to call first for directions.

Best of Both Possible Worlds

ALLENBERRY RESORT INN AND PLAYHOUSE
Boiling Springs, Pennsylvania

Here is the best of the worlds of inning and resorting. A touch of the past and fresh breezes from the present, along with a four hundred-seat playhouse and resident company doing its level best to bring Broadway to Boiling Springs.

The core, preserved to bring guests country inn feelings, consists of a 1785 building and one from 1814. The first contains the dining room; the second has fifteen guest rooms which come closest to being Colonial. The other rooms, rambling away from the center of the campus with its spacious grounds and general feeling of tranquility, are definitely more modern. But then so too are the tennis and badminton courts and the swimming pool, and, for families who want to get away from it all, there is trout fishing in their own stream as well as cottages tucked into shady groves.

ALLENBERRY RESORT INN AND PLAYHOUSE, Box 7, Route 147, Boiling Springs, Pennsylvania 17007. Telephone: (717) 258-3211. Accommodations: 60 rooms; private baths; telephones; televisions. Rates: inexpensive to moderate. Children and pets permitted. Cards: AE, DC, MC, VISA. Closed December through March.

Getting There: From Carlisle follow State Road 34 south to State Road 174; turn left and drive six miles to Boiling Springs.

Cross This Bridge When You Come to It

HICKORY BRIDGE FARM

Orrtana, Pennsylvania

Not a working farm with dairy cows, chickens, hogs to slop; but a working farm in the sense of setting, of stocked bass pond and swimming pool, and of restored and carefully maintained buildings, including a wonderful old barn, all of it lovingly cared for by the Hammett family.

There is trout fishing in a brook that babbles its way through the property, paths for strolling, an annual fall festival when locals and tourists stream in for the leaf season and expect to be fed with some of the fresh bounty of all the nearby farms—and funnel cakes, scrapple, Pennsylvania Dutch sausage, of course.

In proper weather a full-scale country breakfast is served to inn guests on the handsome little deck overlooking the covered bridge, and on Saturday nights there is back-to-the-farm eating with all kinds of solid fare and baked-fresh breads, apple butter and apple dumplings. Monday through Saturday, the farm caters only to groups, to wedding receptions, and the like.

Dining in the century-old barn filled with interesting old farm implements is sheer delight. But then too is overnighting in one of the rooms, in the farmhouse, or in one of the cottages. They too are filled with antiques and interesting accent pieces, braided rugs, quilts, marble-top chests.

HICKORY BRIDGE FARM, 96 Hickory Bridge Road, Orrtana, Pennsylvania 17353. Telephone: (717) 642-5261. Accommodations: seven rooms; six with private baths; no telephones; no televisions. Rates: moderate, includes full breakfast. Children welcome. No pets. Cards: MC, VISA. Closed December 22 through January 1.

Getting There: Orrtana is eight miles west of Gettysburg via U.S. 30 to Cashtown or State Road 116 to Fairfield—watch for signs to the inn.

A Museum of an Inn
FAIRFIELD INN
Fairfield, Pennsylvania

James Monroe was in the White House when this solidly constructed three-story stone blockhouse first welcomed its overnight visitors. Expanded from a 1755 plantation home, the inn was a popular resting place for those weary travelers traversing the stagecoach route which ran from York and Abbotstown to Hagerstown across the border in Maryland.

Those days are vibrantly brought to life in the furnishings, the mementos, the accent pieces overflowing the public and private rooms where drovers by the dozens once raised their steins and filled their stomachs. Innkeeper David Thomas presides over a veritable museum in the old tavern and a neighboring guest house where each of the four accommodations is furnished in a fashion loyal to a particular period of the inn's long history.

A vital part of that past concerns the defeated legions of General Robert E. Lee. Retreating to their Confederate base after the battle of Gettysburg, the troops were given bean soup by the ladies of the inn and town. And today they are still dispensing that hearty brew, along with other solid back-country fare: baked ham, roast chicken served with biscuits dripping with honey, deep-dish apple pies served with the kind of thick cream usually encountered in England, not this country.

The Gettysburg area is unfortunately not as honest as that pie. It is High Tack, commercial kitsch, phony history and there is even a space needle observation tower, all surrounding the National Military Park. But plan your sightseeing around such insults and head straight for the Visitor Center and the splendid Cyclorama Center with its sound and light panoramic view of the events of July, 1863.

More than fifty thousand Americans were killed, wounded or listed as missing in action and many of them are buried in the adjacent National cemetery. There too is the Soldiers' National Monument where President Lincoln delivered his address on November 18, 1863. A draft of that famous speech is displayed during summer months at the Cyclorama Center.

Also in Gettysburg, in the center of the small town, is a splendid Italianate county courthouse with a pedimented portico and an unusual clock tower built the year before the Civil War broke out. Three decades earlier, the first building of the Lutheran Theological Seminary was constructed. It served as hospital for both the blue and the gray, as did nearby Pennsylvania Hall, the 1837 Greek Revival brick building, part of Gettysburg College, the oldest Lutheran college in the nation.

FAIRFIELD INN, 15 West Main Street, Fairfield, Pennsylvania 17320. Telephone: (717) 642-5410. Accommodations: five rooms, four in adjoining guest house; shared baths; no telephones; no televisions. Rates: inexpensive. Children and pets permitted. Cards: MC, VISA. Closed during the month of February and for two weeks in September.

Getting There: The town of Fairfield is eight miles southwest of Gettysburg on State Road 116. The inn is on the town's main street.

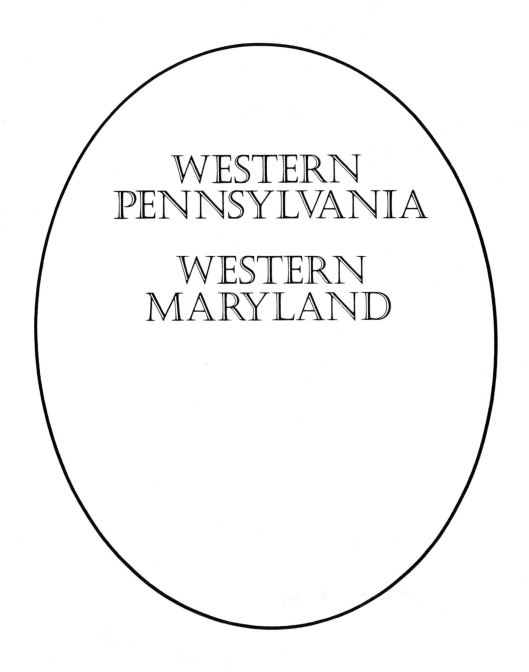

WESTERN
PENNSYLVANIA

WESTERN
MARYLAND

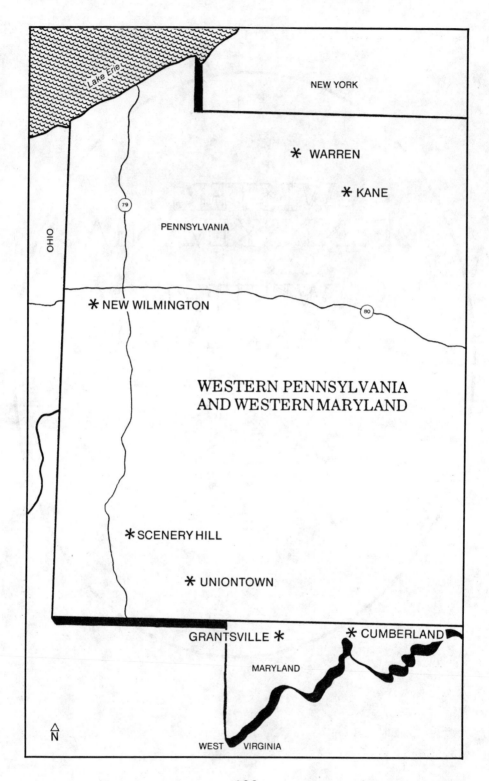

WESTERN PENNSYLVANIA
AND WESTERN MARYLAND

NEW YORK

* WARREN

* KANE

PENNSYLVANIA

OHIO

Lake Erie

* NEW WILMINGTON

* SCENERY HILL

* UNIONTOWN

GRANTSVILLE *

* CUMBERLAND

MARYLAND

WEST   VIRGINIA

△
N

106

WESTERN
PENNSYLVANIA

Memories of a Remarkable Man
KANE MANOR COUNTRY INN
Kane, Pennsylvania

The inn and its town are named for a truly remarkable man, Thomas L. Kane, born in Philadelphia in 1822 of old Revolutionary stock and one of the first Pennsylvanians to volunteer in the Union cause in 1861 A lawyer and son of a federal judge, he was commissioned by the governor to recruit a regiment of mountain sharpshooters. They became famous in battle after battle as the Bucktails. After the war he moved to the northwest reaches of the state, building a log home, taming the wilderness, and developing the rich lumber and then oil and natural gas resources of the area. In 1878 he built the town's first church (he is buried there) and today it is a Historic Site of the Church of Jesus Christ of Latter-Day Saints, beautifully restored and preserved.

General Kane befriended and defended the Mormons, ever since 1846 when he by chance came across the deserted streets and buildings of Nauvoo, Illinois, on the banks of the Mississippi River. Some twelve thousand had been persecuted and forced to flee to Iowa where they were living in migration camps. Kane visited those camps and when he returned east he argued for toleration, petitioning Congress after Brigham Young, his friend, had led his flock into Utah. Kane also fought for prison reform and for the abolition of slavery, participating in the Underground Railroad to smuggle escaped slaves across the border into New York and Canada.

Kane died in 1883; thirteen years later his original home was destroyed by fire and the present manor house was built by his widow and her three sons, who continued their father's development of the area. Today the eighteen thousand square feet of manor is carefully preserved to serve as a charmingly appointed hostelry.

Kane's widow christened the home "Anatoke," an Eskimo word meaning "place that kisses the wind." She no doubt learned this from the General's brother, Elisha K. Kane, who led the Grinnel Arctic expedition of 1850 across some thirteen hundred miles of ice and snow searching for the lost British explorer, Sir John Franklin. Kane became a national hero and original paintings of his exploits are hanging on the inn's walls. There are also books on the subject, along with interesting volumes on Colonial and Civil War history. In the four-thousand-book library in the rathskeller of a pub, the stump tables, made from cross sections of trees, are painted with Elisha Kane's interpretations of various historic events.

Each of the ten guest rooms is individually decorated; largest is the Yellow Room with oversize windows and a window seat. The Blue Room has a sunken tub and overlooks the front gardens; the Garden Room, once an office, has a view of the rose gardens. The old sewing room in dark brown, the nursery, the old master bedroom and a quaint room filled with some of the Kane family's antiques serve as other accommodations. The Summer and Autumn rooms, which share a bath, provide the best views of the valley of Allegheny National Forest.

The Allegheny is the only national forest in the state, surrounding the hundreds of acres of private sanctuary around the inn. The forest runs north all the way to the New York border twenty miles away and is laced with hiking and hunting trails. Not far away is the Kinzua Bridge

D. A. Driscoll

State Park with its abandoned three hundred-foot-high railroad bridge, now used for walking and observing the beauty of the woods. The stream winding through it is noted for trout.

There wasn't any trout on the menu at the manor when last I was there, but the Bucktail Dining Room—named for that famous regiment—did have kabobs of beef and scallops, good veal marsala, and shrimp and chicken elegante, lightly herbed breasts baked in mushroom-freckled wine sauce and served over buttered noodles.

There is more hearty fare to be found during the colder months when the fireplaces are blazing and cross-country skiers assemble, taking advantage of the special package arrangements, the ski rentals and instruction organized by the inn.

KANE MANOR COUNTRY INN, 230 Clay Street, Kane, Pennsylvania 16735. Telephone: (814) 837-6522. Accommodations: 10 rooms; four sharing baths; no telephones; television in rooms. Rates: moderate, includes Continental breakfast weekdays and full breakfast on weekends. Full bar and restaurant service; gift shop. Children permitted. No pets. Cards: AE, MC, VISA. Open all year.

Getting There: The inn is on U.S. 6, a few hundred meters east of the junction of U.S. 6 with State Road 321.

Antique Collector's Paradise
THE WILLOWS
Warren, Pennsylvania

Shannon and Frank Scarpino, antique collectors and dealers from way back, have opened their array of antiques to all those who want to spend a night immersed in the past. Their 1875 three-story white frame house is filled with them: in the rooms and in a shop, and almost all are for sale. Almost all, because there is a fabulous brass bed in one of the guest rooms that is definitely not for sale—it is a family heirloom.

Milliners also will love this place—the collection of hats is sensational. And so is the sense of order, despite all the antiques and collectibles. The Scarpinos run an orderly, neatly maintained, homey kind of inn, one complete with a couple of dogs and a young child.

THE WILLOWS, 40 Kinzua Road, Route 59 Warren, Pennsylvania 16365. Telephone: (814) 726-2667. Accommodations: three rooms; shared bath; no telephones; no televisions. Rates: inexpensive, includes Continental breakfast. Children permitted. No pets. No cards. Open all year.

Getting There: Take U.S. 6 east from Warren to the junction with State Road 59 leading to the Kinzua Dam; drive 2.4 miles on 59; on the right side of the highway is the inn.

Happy Valley Heartland
THE TAVERN LODGE
New Wilmington, Pennsylvania

This is really an urban inn, located in the heart of a city—or rather village, for New Wilmington with buggies of Amish farmers clip-clopping across its streets, is only relatively urban. Thus the fact that inn and restaurant are smack in the center of town, with one located on East Neshannock on one side of Market Street and the other on West Neshannock a few feet away on the other side, does not mean a bustling, noisy atmosphere.

Neshannock comes from the name of the stream which, with the rivers Mahoning and Shenango (other marvelous Indian sounds), form a branch of Beaver Valley which the locals have dubbed Happy Valley—although to mining interests it is simply Tionesta sandstone, yielding iron-bearing limestone, coal and gas.

New Wilmington, named after Wilmington in England, was founded in 1797 on land that the Delaware Indians, the Mingoes and the Senecas once roamed freely. Forty years later this inn was built as a home by a local doctor, Seth Poppino, surgeon in the Union Army. In 1950 the Durrasts took over, transforming it into an inn and restaurant with six dining rooms furnished in Colonial style, each with fireplace. On weekends the staff, mostly students from high school and college, is garbed in Colonial dress. Menus are also Colonial—recited verbally—and consist of plain farm foods: fried and roast chicken, steak, some seafood and always the fresh-baked honey rolls. The rooms are a few feet away across Market Street, and are similarly Colonial and vibrant with a sense of history.

110

For more history, tour Johnston's Tavern, eight miles from town: once a stagecoach stop, it is a two-story stone structure providing food and lodging that was put up by an Irish immigrant named Arthur Johnston—he called it the New Lodge Inn. It was on the old Pittsburgh-Mercer Road (now Route 19) and was a station on the Underground Railroad. As was Dr. Poppino's home and the so-called Ten-Sided House a mile east of New Bedford on Marr Road. Also known as the Roundhouse, its polygon construction was supposed to decrease wind penetration. A much smaller building is the Cheesehouse, two miles west of New Wilmington at the intersection of Routes 18 and 208. It is small, but that is only the sales area. Next door, in this important dairy land, is what they declare to be the largest Swiss cheese factory in the world. Closer to the inn is Westminster College, founded by the Associate Presbyterian Church in 1852, one of the first co-educational institutions in the country.

THE TAVERN LODGE, 101 N. Market Street, New Wilmington, Pennsylvania 16142. Telephone: (412) 946-2091. Accommodations: five rooms; private baths; no telephones; television in rooms. Rates: inexpensive. Children permitted. Pets permitted. No cards. Open all year.

Getting There: The inn is in the center of town, at the intersection of Market (State Roads 158 and 956) and Neshannock (State Road 208).

On a Clear Day You Can See Forever
CENTURY INN
Scenery Hill, Pennsylvania

They could call this collection of antiques the two-century inn: it has been dispensing hospitality to travelers since 1794. General Lafayette breakfasted here when making his triumphal tour of the country in 1825; Andrew Jackson spent the night when making his way east to his inauguration as President. They were both traveling the National Road, today's U.S. 40, paved over an ancient Indian path which was also used by young Colonel Washington when he led his Virginia militia into battle with the French and Indians.

It is the oldest continuously operated inn on the Old Pike and, thanks to the dedication and tireless collecting zeal of its owners, the inn is one of the best furnished of any in the land. Gordon and Mary Harrington, who breathed new life into the solid stone structure after purchasing it in 1945, were succeeded by another generation of their family who proved to be as devoted in their caretaking responsibilities as their parents. After all, they are operating a building which is on the National Register of Historic Places, one with a rare flag used by the insurrectionists in the Whiskey Rebellion at nearby Monongahela, one filled with all kinds of memories of the past, from long-barrel muskets to dolls and toys.

The original massive fireplace in the kitchen still has its original hand-forged crane and an array of antique utensils; elsewhere are folk art paintings, tools and handicrafts, and restored stencils, and there are more valuable pieces in the individual guest rooms. The front porch, with those gleaming white pillars, is framed by carefully tended gardens and filled with rockers to while away lazy afternoons and appreciate the foresight of Stephen Hill, who founded the aptly named town and built the inn. Gazing out the windows at the wide expanse of forests marching up and down the hills, at the farm buildings dotting the landscape, one has no trouble understanding why he chose the name Scenery Hill.

Maybe on a clear day you could see forever. And on any day you can eat forever, starting with a solid breakfast in that dining room overlooking the countryside; continuing with a lunch of shepherds pie, chicken croquettes, Welsh rarebit, chicken à la king served on waffles, or a ham and asparagus roll; but saving some room for the dinner entrées of stuffed pork chops, roast turkey, scallops and shrimp, and the pies, cheesecake, strawberry shortcake.

CENTURY INN, Route 40, Scenery Hill, Pennsylvania 15360. Telephone: (412) 945-6600. Accommodations: six rooms; private baths; no telephones; no televisions. Rates: inexpensive. Children permitted. No pets. No cards. Open March 1 through mid-December.

Getting There: Scenery Hill and its impossible-to-miss inn are on U.S. 40, twelve miles southeast of Washington, Pennsylvania.

George Washington Did Not Sleep Here

MOUNT SUMMIT INN
Uniontown, Pennsylvania

The panorama views from this aptly named inn are sensational, from guestrooms, from the porches and patios, from the inn's own golf course—above the clouds, and from the tennis, croquet and shuffleboard courts. It is really more of a resort than quiet little country inn, but the location is so unique, the accommodations so comfortable, and the facilities on their nine hundred acres so varied, including indoor and outdoor pools, that I'm stretching definitions a bit to bring the Mount Summit into the book.

There is another reason: the inn is close to Fort Necessity, the name of a hastily constructed fortification ordered built by a twenty-two-year old Lt. Colonel, appointed by Colonial Governor Dinwiddie to confront the French moving into frontier lands from Fort Niagara.

George Washington was that colonel and on May 28, 1754 he launched the French and Indian War, known in Europe as the Seven Years War, with a surprise attack on the encampment of French troops under the command of the Sieur de Jumonville, Joseph Coulon de Villiers. The site of the battle can be visited today—it is three miles north of U.S. 40. Five miles west is Fort Necessity, the palisade fort manned by Washington's Virginia militia, aided by a hundred volunteers from South Carolina and nine swivel guns. On July 3, the French forces counter-attacked and after a day of musket and mortar fire—in a downpour—a truce was negotiated and Washington withdrew, without his swivel guns. The young colonel and his men trudged back to Alexandria and the French destroyed the fort; but it has been reconstructed and there is a fine little visitor center explaining the challenges met in that reconstruction. The ten-minute slide show puts the confrontation of French and English—each with Indian allies—into a proper perspective.

During the summer, June until Labor Day, park rangers give guided tours of this national park and in the spring there are wildflower walks. Washington Tavern, built in the 1820s on a prominence overlooking Fort Necessity, is open all year. It provides valuable insights into the innings of yore, of those days when pioneers heading west into the Ohio Valley traversed the Old National Road. Furnished with period pieces, the inn also has a Conestoga wagon on display.

It sits squarely on U.S. 40, paved primarily over the route of the Old National Road, that wheel-worn artery carved out of the mountain fastness, and a path taken by Washington and his men. In 1755 it was the trail used by General Edward Braddock, leading some thirteen hundred troops against the French at Fort Duquesne. Eight miles from that fort, in the battle of Monongahela, Braddock and some nine hundred of his men were killed or wounded. He died during the hasty retreat and was buried by his men alongside the trail. A half century later, remains said to be his were discovered by workmen and re-interred on a grassy knoll a mile west of Fort Necessity. There is a marker and a plaque explaining the campaign and his defeat.

When the Braddock cum Washington cum Indian trail was converted to National Road, the country's first, it was the Swiss-born financier Albert Gallatin who was responsible. Secretary of the Treasury for both Jefferson and Madison, he also built a fine country home, Friendship Hill, southwest of Fort Necessity on U.S. 119 near Point Marion, now a National Historic Site, open to the public.

There is so much history in these few square miles, a class inn with all the comforts simply has to be included in this book.

MOUNT SUMMIT INN, P.O. Drawer T, Uniontown, Pennsylvania 15401. Telephone: (412) 438-8594. Accommodations: 126 rooms; private baths; telephones; televisions. Rates: moderate with several package deals available, includes breakfast and dinner on modified American plan. Children and pets permitted. No cards. Open May 1– November 1.

Getting There: The inn is 5.5 miles east of Uniontown on U.S. 40.

WESTERN
MARYLAND

Mennonite Mastery
THE CASSELMAN INN
Grantsville, Maryland

When this solidly built structure first opened its doors as the Drover's Inn, it was to serve as stopover for travelers on the National Road seeking their fortune and fame out west. That was 1824 and the innkeeper was one Solomon Sterner. Today the innkeepers are Ivan J. Miller and his hard-working wife Della, who oversee a kitchen which bakes wonderful breads on a daily basis as well as pumpkin and oatmeal cakes and cookies. They also prepare the kind of solid fare one expects to find in an Amish Mennonite community: honey-dipped chicken, unbelieveably honest potatoes and fresh vegetables, smoked sausages and great apple butter which is just begging to be spread over some of that fresh, warm bread.

Miller's great-grandfather operated the inn during the War Between the States. His father was born in the inn, which through the years has been known as Sterner's Tavern, Farmer's Hotel, Dorsey's Hotel and finally as the Casselman, named for the nearby river with its eighty-foot stone arch bridge. This bridge was the longest in the country when it was constructed in 1813 and it was made a Registered Historical Landmark in 1964. That is the year Ivan and his wife took over the inn, adding a modern motel-style unit to the rear and filling each room with furniture hand-crafted by local members of the Mennonite community, for which Ivan serves as bishop.

The inn and its National Road were the chief factors in the development of the town. But the railroad and then the super highways by-passed the village, which sits squarely on one of the most historic thoroughfares in the country. Originally it was an old Indian trail, Nemacolin's Path, traveled by a young Virginia officer pursuing the

Indians—George Washington. General Braddock converted it to military passage, and for years it was the only artery connecting the east with the rich, developing lands of the Ohio Valley. When Congress appropriated funds to rebuild it all the way from Cumberland to Wheeling, it became the first National Pike in the nation.

I like to contemplate that history when I walk around this quiet little country town, twenty-three hundred feet high in the mountains, and when I enter the inn with its heavy, hand-hewn timbers, its wide plank floors and the brick which was baked in the area. And I think of it when I picnic—with sandwiches and cookies brought from the inn, of course—by the ever-so-photogenic Casselman River Bridge, or when I get away from it all in the nearby woods at the New Germany State Park or the Savage River State Forest.

When I return I can sit once again on one of those relaxing rockers in the old inn sitting room, look at those ancient German Bibles in the glass case, stare into the roaring fire, grateful for the inn's lack of catalogue-cute furnishings, wondering once again where they ever got the name Whopee Pie, for those extra-large, puffy cookies made of pumpkin layered with white icing.

CASSELMAN INN, P.O. Box 299 Main Street (U.S. 40), Grantsville, Maryland 21536. Telephone: (301) 895-5055. Accommodations: forty rooms in new motel; private baths; telephones and televisions; five rooms in inn; two with private baths; no televisions. Full meal service. Children permitted. No pets. No cards. Open all year.

Getting There: Grantsville is on U.S. 40, the main street of the town. The inn is in the center of town, impossible to miss. The Grantsville Exit of U.S. 48 is a couple blocks from the inn.

Victorian Town with a Colonial Past

COLONIAL MANOR

Cumberland, Maryland

The Colonial origins go back to the time when Colonel George Washington, aide-de-camp to British General Braddock, was at Fort Cumberland planning skirmishes and raids against the French and Indians. When Washington returned four decades later, it was as President of an independent nation and he was performing his last military act: inspecting the troops gathered to suppress the Pennsylvania farmers in the ill-fated Whiskey Rebellion across the border. The cabin he used as headquarters is all that remains of the old fort and is located on Green Street in the town's Riverside Park.

Successors in the presidency also paid attention to Cumberland. In Jefferson's administration, the town became the gateway to the west as the first federal funds in our history were appropriated to build a National Road, otherwise known as the Cumberland Road, which followed an old Indian trail as well as the military road General Braddock ordered carved out of the thick woods.

When John Quincy Adams was president, he turned the first spade of earth for the new Chesapeake and Ohio Canal, which was to run some 185 miles from Georgetown, by the nation's capital, all the way to Cumberland. That was in 1828. It was not completed until 1850 after an expenditure of $22 million and the construction of a dozen stone aqueducts, seven dams, waste weirs, carry roads and culverts, a three thousand-foot tunnel, locks, bridges, houses, and towpath. The story is all told at the Chesapeake and Ohio Canal National Historical Park at North Branch, five miles south of town. There is a full-scale replica of a canal boat, a log cabin lock house, and guided tours which run from June through August. During the last full weekend in August there is a Canal Boat Festival at the site, which is old Lock 75.

About the time the energetic engineers were completing their canal (eight years after the Baltimore & Ohio Railroad reached Cumberland), a tavern was being constructed of locally made brick and hand-cut timbers held in place with hand-forged nails. The site selected was known as Turkey Flight and that is what the locals dubbed the hostelry. During the Civil War a cannonball blasted its way into the building during the skirmish at nearby Flock's Mill. The wounded were removed to the tavern and their scribblings can still be seen on attic walls. There are other reminders on walls as well as in the construction

117

of the original parts of the inn. Two wings have been added and the guest rooms—a dozen of them executed in a fitting Colonial style and entered via Elizabeth Arden-red doors.

But in the dining room of the Manor the words spell "Stracciatella," "Insalata Capriciosa," "Fettuccine Alfredo," "Saltimbocca," "Calamari," and "Scaloppine al Marsala." Why not? The British, the Colonials, the Indians and the Irish who dug the canal, have been replaced by the Italians—the Gigliottis, Maria and Oswald, known as "Oz." Their restaurant L'Osteria, is a winner, one with a splendid little wine cellar/lounge serving luncheons and lighter fare and providing weekend entertainment.

There are other enclaves of exotica in the area, ranging from German to Chinese, including a favorite for all frankfurter freaks. In town, near the impossible-to-miss Cumberland Mall is a storefront announcing that they sell "Curtis Wieners, Famous Since 1918." They dollop them with genuine Coney Island sauce: a few pounds of chili and onions.

Take some along when you start your in-town touring around the Washington Street Historic District, with its fine mix of nineteenth-century home styles. But first pick up a brochure so you don't mix up Queen Anne with Colonial Revival, Italianate with Second Empire, Greek Revival or something in-between. Brochures, and much else of interest, are found at the History House at 218 Washington. A Second Empire mansion with Victorian furnishings, it was built in 1867 and now contains Civil War memorabilia, along with toys and costumes and early medical instruments. The Bicentennial Garden close by is lovely and beyond it is the Carriage House, with its early fire equipment and other vehicles.

When leaving Cumberland, travel west on U.S. 40 six miles to LaVale and its Toll Gate House, open to visitors May through August. A seven-sided oddity complete with cupola, it was the first toll house constructed on the National Road—and is the only one remaining in the state.

COLONIAL MANOR, U.S. 40 East (Route 2, Box 109), Cumberland, Maryland 21502. Telephone: (301) 777-3553. Accommodations: 12 rooms; private baths; telephones; televisions. Rates: inexpensive. Full bar service; lunch and dinner. Children permitted. Inquire about pets. Cards: AE, MC, VISA. Open all year.

Getting There: The inn is three miles east of downtown Cumberland on the main road, U.S. 40.

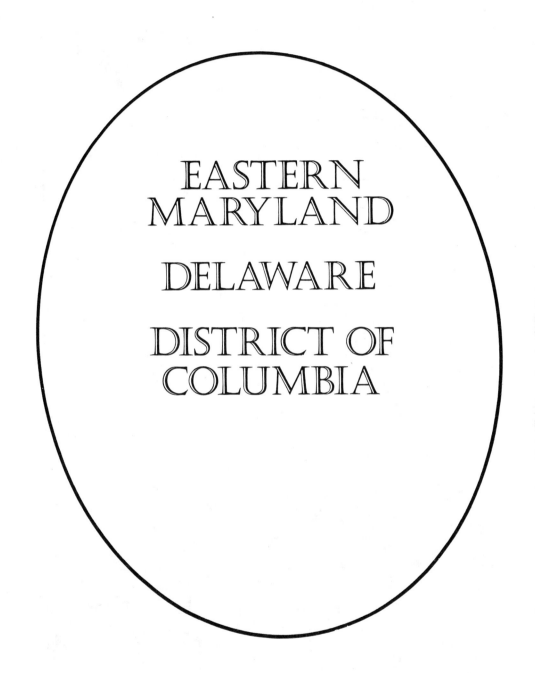

EASTERN
MARYLAND

DELAWARE

DISTRICT OF
COLUMBIA

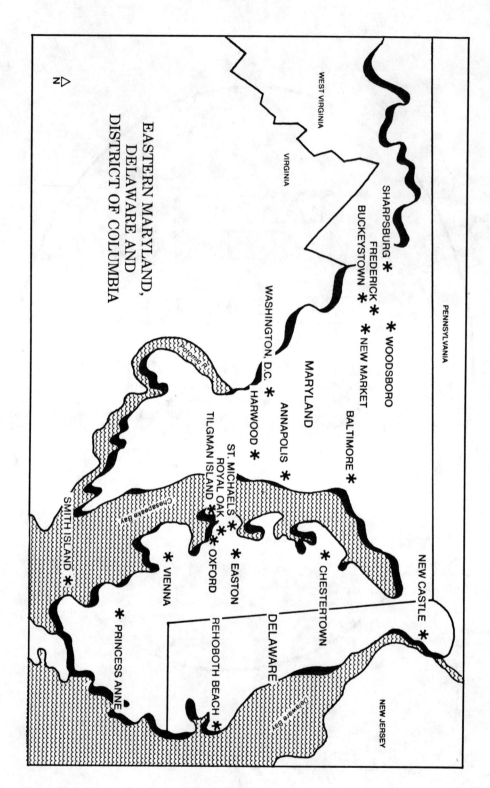

EASTERN MARYLAND,
DELAWARE AND
DISTRICT OF COLUMBIA

N

PENNSYLVANIA

WEST VIRGINIA

VIRGINIA

SHARPSBURG *
FREDERICK *
BUCKEYSTOWN *

* WOODSBORO
* NEW MARKET

MARYLAND

WASHINGTON, D.C. *

Potomic R.

BALTIMORE *

HARWOOD *

ANNAPOLIS *

ST. MICHAELS
ROYAL OAK
TILGMAN ISLAND
OXFORD *
EASTON *

CHESTERTOWN *

Chesapeake Bay

SMITH ISLAND *

VIENNA *

PRINCESS ANNE *

DELAWARE

REHOBOTH BEACH *

Delaware Bay

NEW CASTLE *

NEW JERSEY

120

EASTERN
MARYLAND

The Calm after the Storm
INN AT ANTIETAM
Sharpsburg, Maryland

Civil War buffs of course know all about this area. It is where General Robert E. Lee and his brave band of Confederates, their lines of supply over-extended and their forces vastly outnumbered by the legions in blue under the command of General George McClellan, were decimated. The Battle of Antietam was the bloodiest day of the War Between the States—in fact, the bloodiest day in American military history. When the last shot was fired on September 17, 1862, some 24,500 men lay dead in the fields and farms alongside Bloody Lane, by Burnside Bridge and Dunkard Church. It was the beginning of the end for the South.

The Antietam National Battlefield, a twelve-square-mile spread joined by winding roads and clearly marked signs indicating deployment of forces, is best viewed by car today. Take the Hagerstown Pike to the Visitor Center, which has maps as well as a superb collection of Civil War pieces.

Innkeeper Betty Fairbourn can point the way from the wonderful wraparound porch of her turn-of-the-century rambling Victorian inn. Her inn, with its cozy, ultra-clean guestrooms, is right on the battlefield, right on the main street of Sharpsburg, next to the cemetary. That front porch is a restful retreat after driving and walking over the site, where so many gave their lives, or visiting the other unique destinations in the area. A mile and a half northeast of the inn at Snyder's Landing is the Chesapeake & Ohio Canal Museum. A little farther northeast is Boonsboro, with Maryland's only caverns open to the public, as well as the Scoper House Museum, devoted to the history of the town, its Indian origins and its role in the Civil War.

Near Boonsboro on Alternate U.S. 40 is the entrance to the Washington Monument State Park with its minimuseum, access to the Appalachian Trail and the first monument erected to our first president which was dedicated on the Fourth of July, 1827. Across the entrance to the park is the Old South Mountain Inn, a time-worn stone fortress dating from 1730 and still serving the public.

Some ten miles north of Sharpsburg is Hagerstown with the Price-Miller House, a nineteenth-century museum filled with various crafts exhibits, an army of dolls and numerous clocks. There is also the Jonathan Hager House and Museum, a two and one-half story 1740 restored reminder of the days of the town's founder.

The Fairbourns can direct their guests to any and all of the places that must be seen while staying in their inn. They are also happy to route their incoming guests away from the cities and the traffic. Washington, D.C. is only ninety minutes away, but rather than relying on the beltways and thruways of that congestion, the Fairbourns like to have their guests see some of the beauties of the Maryland-Virginia-West Virginia countryside. They also make sure their guests, once in place, are fully satisfied. "Betty Fairbourn," proclaims her husband with considerable pride, "makes the best breakfast in town." She also has the best inn in town.

INN AT ANTIETAM, 220 East Main Street (P.O. Box 119), Sharpsburg, Maryland 21782. Telephone: (301) 432-6601. Accommodations: four rooms; one with sitting room; two with private baths; no telephones; no televisions. Rates: moderate, includes full breakfast. Inquire about children. No pets. No cards. Open all year.

Getting There: The inn is on the main street of the small town, next door to the military cemetary.

Inn at Antietam

BED AND BOARD AT TRAN CROSSING
Frederick, Maryland

Georgetown North is what Frederick is often called in the greater Washington area. And for good reason. The restoration of grand Georgian, Federal and Colonial homes and the revitalization of ancient churches and buildings converted into shops which appeal to all tastes and pocketbooks has been in progress for the past several years. And in the heart of it all, the Trans, Becky and Fred, have made it possible for visitors to immerse themselves in the history and to be near all the shopping and strolling action. They have fully renovated a three-story townhouse, a nineteenth-century Victorian flat-front gem, which they keep in immaculate condition. The downstairs rooms are filled with antiques while the second floor guest rooms, which are reached by a winding stairway which grandly swirls, are slightly more modern. The Trans made the comfort of their guests their main concern when furnishing their crossing.

One of the rooms has a fold-out sofa in the sitting area, and there is a jib window with a fine view of the town and its several church steeples. The bathroom is shared, but that bath, as high-ceilinged as the bedrooms on its flanks, is large enough for a family reunion.

An ample Continental breakfast is included and for an extra charge a full-blown Southern spread is arranged: eggs and meat, muffins, biscuits and breads, and grits or German fries. Served in the dining room or in the garden, it is wonderful stoking for a day of exploring Georgetown North.

Start the tour a block away on Church Street at the Visitor's Center, next door to the Evangelical Lutheran Church, which was initially built in 1738 and then rebuilt in 1855. There the tourist can pick up maps, brochures and walking tour sheets; or arrange for guided tours. Around the corner from Church Street is the City Hall and the Old Opera House. This is where the town fathers had to pay a ransom of $200 thousand to Confederate General Jubal Early so that he would spare the town. Early's forces had defeated the Yankees under General Lew Wallace (who after the war wrote *Ben Hur*) at the Battle of Monocacy three miles south of town.

Two years earlier, another Confederate General rode through town—Stonewall Jackson. And if one can believe the heroic poetry of John Greenleaf Whittier, it was Jackson who looked up to Barbara

Fritchie defiantly waving her Union flag and declared, "Who touches a hair on yon gray head/Dies like a dog! March on!" The poem, the story, is remembered in the Barbara Fritchie Museum a few doors from Tran Crossing.

Also close at hand is Trinity Chapel, built in 1764 and the place where Francis Scott Key was baptized. He is buried in the town's Mount Olivet Cemetery at the southern end of Market Street, and a number of his possessions are preserved in the Roger Brooke Taney Home and Francis Scott Key Museum on South Bentz Street. Taney, a Supreme Court justice most noted for his Dred Scott decision, was Key's brother-in-law.

On North Market Street is Rose Hill Manor, built just before the Revolution and the retirement home of Maryland's first governor, Thomas Johnson. Now it is a children's museum of history. Not far away is the Historical Society with its own collection of dolls, Indian artifacts and exhibits on the history of the town.

BED AND BOARD AT TRAN CROSSING, 121 East Patrick Street, Frederick, Maryland 21701. Telephone: (301) 663-8449. Accommodations: two rooms sharing one bath; no telephones; no television. Rates: moderate, includes Continental breakfast. Children permitted. No pets. No cards. Open all year.

Getting There: Patrick Street is the old National Pike, reached from Exit 7 of U.S. 15. From Exit 7, take Rosemont Avenue a couple blocks east to College Avenue, turn south (right) four blocks to Patrick.

A Rose Is a Rose Is a Rose

THE ROSEBUD INN
Woodsboro, Maryland

Gertrude Stein should have visited Woodsboro when she penned that immortal line. Here a rose is an inn, a rose is a perfume company, a rose is a salve, and there are roses cut into the beautiful stained glass windows of this Colonial Revival home built for the man who loved roses, Dr. George F. Smith.

Next door to that home, which in 1980 was carefully restored and reborn as the Rosebud Inn, Smith had his Rosebud Perfume Company. His grandchildren still operate the mail order business, shipping their perfume, Rosebud Salve and Strawberry Lip Balm all over the world. Looking through the windows of that concern, it is hard to believe that the good doctor is not somewhere in residence, measuring or bottling or wrapping. There is a time-stood-still museum air about the place.

I felt the same way about the town, which seems to be frozen in the nineteenth century. Close by the inn is a furniture company which specializes in dollhouses; the old five-story grist mill, with its original machinery, houses an antique store; and the most exciting activity in town is the Tuesday livestock sales and flea market. But in June there is the annual Fireman's Carnival, with country music and fun for the kids, and in October the town puts on a steam show, complete with a tractor pulling contest.

Alice and Albert Eaton, innkeepers at the helm of the Rosebud since they bought the property in 1980, understand that laid back, ole-

timey spirit of Woodsboro. And in their inn they strive to keep that spirit alive. The public rooms are filled with antiques and lacy table coverings, the massive marble mantels and the Colonial-style worked woodwork have been carefully maintained, and everywhere there is evidence of very fussy care and concern.

At the end of the day guests sit in the living room with fireplace blazing, exchanging stories about the day's excursions—to New Market for its antiques; Frederick for its history and its Civil War memories; Catoctin Mountain National Park for picnicking, nature hiking and handicraft demonstrations; or Emmitsburg where there is the Grotto of Lourdes founded by Saint Elizabeth Ann Seton, America's first saint. Sitting there, the guest is tempted to get on the mailing list for some of that Rosebud Perfume or lip balm.

THE ROSEBUD INN, 4 North Main Street, Woodsboro, Maryland 21798. Telephone: (301) 845-2221. Accommodations: five rooms; 3 with private baths; no telephones; no television. Rates: moderate, includes Continental breakfast. No children. No pets. Cards: MC, VISA. Open all year.

Getting There: Woodsboro is nine miles northeast of Frederick on State Road 194; the inn is on the main street of the town.

Innkeepers Who Are Involved
THE INN AT BUCKEYSTOWN
Buckeystown, Maryland

This 1897 Victorian mansion has been an inn only since 1982, but Daniel Pelz and Marty Martinez have furnished their multi-story rambling empire with such care and concern that one has the feeling guests have been coming to this out-of-the-way place forever.

For years Dan wanted his own inn. As he tours his guests happily through his domain he redefines the title of innkeeper again and again, always going the extra steps—placing a rose on the dinner plate of a guest celebrating an anniversary, preparing a special dish he knows a repeat visitor favors. In addition to his other innkeeping responsibilities, Dan puts in a good many hours in the kitchen as does partner Marty. Together they produce an interesting combination of culinary traditions, Dan reflecting his Pennsylvania Dutch background, Marty his Spanish.

Thus, a dinner (and a family dinner along with full country breakfast is always part of the room rate at this inn) might start with a pumpkin soup heightened by chopped green onions and fresh dill, move on to a fillet of meat given the Basque garlic treatment or veal medallions lightly kissed with a heavy cream sauce, and then finish with a sinfully delicious dessert.

Between the 8:30 a.m. bountiful breakfasts and the 7 p.m. dinners, the visitor to Buckeystown can while away the hours on the grand old wraparound porch or stroll the two and one-half acre gardens searching for the Civil War cemetery. Buckeystown is in the center of much of the Civil War action in these parts and Harper's Ferry, the Monocacy Battlefield and Gettysburg are close by. Within easy driving distance is Antietam, site of the bloodiest day in United States military history.

Returning to the happily kept inn, one is treated like a member of the family, greeted at table and provided with setups for the BYOB arrangements. Then, after a hearty meal and much good conversation, one retires to the second- and third-floor guestrooms, walking up that splendid oak-paneled staircase, past the rather ornate crystal chandeliers, and into the individually decorated rooms, each with its own decanter of port, some fruit, an ample supply of reading material, and one or more representations of a clown. There will be a crocheted clown on the pillow and some prints, photos or magazine covers on the walls.

A favorite room here is the one with a carpet into which the word *love* has been woven—which, of course, is the Love Room. It, like the others, has carefully selected towels to blend in with the colors of the room. The accent pieces will also be a welcome addition to the visitor seeking a touch of the homefront while traveling. They provide as special a feeling of elegant Victoriana as the heavy silver, the elaborate china and the crystal which is used morn and night.

THE INN AT BUCKEYSTOWN, 3521 Buckeystown Pike, Buckeystown, Maryland 21717. Telephone: (301) 874-5755. Accommodations: six rooms; shared baths; no telephones; no televisions. Rates: moderate, includes dinner and full breakfast. No children. No pets. Cards: MC and VISA, but prefer personal check. Open all year.

Getting There: From Frederick and Interstate 270, take the Buckeystown Exit, State Road 85, five miles directly to the town and its inn on the main street.

Antique Hunters Heaven

THE STRAWBERRY INN
New Market, Maryland

There cannot be more than four hundred residents on this sleepy stretch of road midway between Baltimore and Frederick, but there are close to half a hundred antique stores. Most are in buildings that have been carefully rescued from the past and proudly made to serve the present. The town's Main Street used to be on the National Pike, and the six-horse Conestoga wagons once were a common sight rolling westward into Ohio territory and other unknown parts. Today this street is part of the Historic District, which was placed in the National Register a decade ago, and includes the very plot of land laid out for the town in 1793 by William Plummer and Nicholas Hall.

For five days a week the town is about as quiet as it was after railroads and highways passed it by and left it forgotten in this century, but now on the weekends the streets are filled with antique hunters who swarm from Baltimore, Washington and even New York and Philadelphia. The only overnight accommodation they can find in town is at the Strawberry Inn which is hardly a many-roomed Hilton.

There are only five guest rooms in the strawberry-colored house with its center gable peak and its sweet little front porch, with a general appearance of having been built to house dolls, not people. Inside, all is antique, and the innkeepers, Ed and Jane Rossig, have selected with restraint and with great good taste. The rooms are exquisitely furnished with coordinated colors, brass beds and modern tiled bathrooms. An overall sense of quiet and calm prevails, intended by the Rossigs to be "a place to re-establish your identity and return home with good thoughts."

Continental breakfasts are delivered to rooms on butler's trays and for lunch and dinner there is an old inn across Main Street known as Mealey's. It's been serving the public since 1916 and while they no longer have overnight accommodations, they do have a cozy bar in the front, candlelight and family-style dinners featuring crab imperial, shrimp and other seafood, chicken, steak, and good old country ham.

The town, which has christened itself, with no little justification, the Antiques Capital of Maryland, has an annual festival, New Market Days, the last weekend in September. The second Friday in December there is a Christmas celebration and other than that, the biggest news in town consists of occasional pancake breakfasts and a New Year's Eve dance, both sponsored by the New Market Volunteer Fire Company.

THE STRAWBERRY INN, 17 Main Street (P.O. Box 237), New Market, Maryland 21774. Telephone: (301) 865-3318. Accommodations: five rooms; private baths; no telephones; no televisions. Rates: inexpensive, includes Continental breakfast. Children over seven preferred. No pets. No cards. Open all year.

Getting There: From Interstate 70 take Exit 60 to New Market; the inn is on the town's Main Street, impossible to miss.

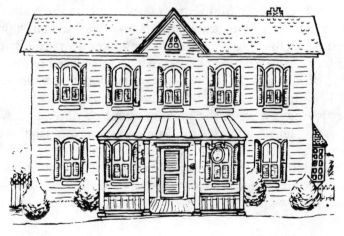

Urban Inn
SOCIETY HILL
Baltimore, Maryland

The tireless trio that created what they call an urban inn in the heart of Philadelphia, Thomas Kleinman, David DeGraff and Judith Campbell, each a veteran of far larger hotel corporations, decided to clone their operation elsewhere. What worked so successfully in Philadelphia might find similar enthusiasm in another Eastern Seabord city—Baltimore.

They found their neighborhood in the Mount Vernon District, which around the time the nation was fragmenting into opposite camps before the Civil War, was *the* place to live. It had once belonged to a hero of the Revolution, Colonel John Eager Howard, who set aside a portion of it as a tribute with fitting memorial to his revered commander-in-chief, George Washington.

Today the district is again coming to life with the sophisticated set returning to the city and with tourists seeking out Harborplace, the aquarium, and the fort, whose mighty battle inspired Francis Scott Key to write the "Star Spangled Banner." Symphony Hall is right across the street from the urban inn and the Lyric Opera and the Institute of Art are close by. Within an easy stroll is that several-block spread of specialty shops known as Antique Row.

Some of these stores might have been the source of the brass beds, the heavy wooden furniture and the handsome accent pieces that Kleinman, DeGraff, and Campbell found for the guest rooms. They have combined the best of the old and the new in a cozy at-home atmosphere highly prized by the tourist or the business visitor eager to avoid the chain reactions of the plastic, fresh-from-the-catalogue settings of so many other accommodations.

What this trio started in Philadelphia (described in this book) in 1981 has successfully been repeated a little farther south. Can other eastern cities be far behind? Will they also add a restaurant and a jazz piano bar and the kind of bounteous Sunday brunch that they established in Baltimore? Why not? One good urban inn deserves another.

SOCIETY HILL, 58 West Biddle Street, Baltimore, Maryland, 21201. Telephone: (301) 837-3630. Accommodations: 15 rooms; private baths; telephones and televisions. Rates: expensive, includes Continental breakfast. Full bar and meal service. Children over 8 permitted. No pets. Cards: AE, DC, MC, VISA. Open all year.

Getting There: Biddle Street runs parallel to Chase and Preston; the inn is between Cathedral and Maryland Avenues. Take U.S. 40 to Park Avenue and turn left onto Biddle.

A Salute from Savannah

ADMIRAL FELL INN
Baltimore, Maryland

The origins of this inn dominating Fells Point, the original site of Baltimore, go back to that early era as well as the eighteenth century, when a series of waterfront buildings were constructed and then added to over the years. But the idea for transforming the brick and stone to something liveable go back only a few years and originate in Savannah, Georgia.

Baltimore Mayor William Donald Schafer visited Savannah and stayed at the Eliza Thompson House in that fair city. The Eliza Thompson was one of the first of the city inns magically converted from an ancient and honorable home, and it occupies a prized place in my *Country Inns of the Old South.* The Widmans, energetic and imaginative innkeepers, were convinced by the Mayor that they should work the same kind of wonder in his city. After a couple of years of strenuous restoration efforts and finding the kind of antiques and collectibles they wanted for furnishings, and a staff to take over restaurant and lounge, they opened the Admiral Fell, just in time to make this guidebook.

The location is enviable. On Market Square alongside the waterfront, the inn is close to Johns Hopkins Hospital, the Convention center and Fort McHenry. Nearby is Charles Center, the company whose spices render a special aroma in its proximity (and which gives tours), and of course Harborplace with all its attractions, on and off the water, and all those eating and buying temptations.

The Admiral Fell has its own delights to tempt its guests: a cozy pub and a handsome restaurant, a splendid observation deck and courtyard, an atrium, and even a small library, providing inngoers with a corner of civilized refuge.

ADMIRAL FELL INN, 888 South Broadway, Baltimore, Maryland 21231. Telephone: (301) 522-7377. Accommodations: 37 rooms; private baths; telephones; color televisions. Rates: expensive, includes Continental breakfast. Full bar and meal service. Children permitted. No pets. Cards: AE, MC, VISA. Open all year.

Getting There: Getting there: The inn is on Market Square at Thames Street at Fells Point by the harbor.

Perfect Place for Perfect Inn
MARYLAND INN
Annapolis, Maryland

If ever an inn has been situated in the perfect place to complement its own history and sense of place, it is the Maryland Inn in Annapolis. Everywhere are carefully restored, lovingly maintained echoes of the past of the town that was so vital during Colonial times: as port, as the country's first peacetime capital, as home of the Naval Academy. Within view is the wooden dome of the State House, listed on the National Register of Historic Places and located in the heart of the Annapolis Historic District. The Treaty of Paris was ratified under that dome, ending the Revolutionary War. General George Washington, in the great tradition of Cincinnatus, resigned his commission as Commander-in-Chief of the Continental Army and a bronze plaque marks the precise spot where he stood. Edwin White captured the scene on canvas and this painting now hangs in the State House. Charles Wilson Peale's rendition of Washington at the Battle of Yorktown also hangs there: Maryland hero Tench Tilghman (as in Tilghman Island) is depicted as well.

The 1780 State House, arguably the most beautiful building in the country, is the oldest capitol in continuous use. Its near neighbor, the Maryland Inn, qualifies as one of the oldest hostelries in continuous use as well. Built on a triangular wedge of land that had originally been set aside for the use of the Annapolis Town Drummer, it was later purchased by a local merchant, Thomas Hyde, who built an inn, with twenty-two rooms and twenty fireplaces in the 1770s. A century later a fourth floor was built, and over the years modern conveniences have been added, but always with a close eye to retaining the reminders of the Colonial past.

133

Even in the public rooms, the Drummer's Lot Taproom, the Treaty of Paris room and the King of France Tavern, which opened in 1784 and today features the likes of the Charlie Byrd Trio, Art Hodes and Monty Alexander, the sense of history and place is retained. I found this heady atmosphere while surveying the inn's property and admiring the Colonial craftmanship in the wooden panels, cornices, mantels and fireplaces.

This feeling persists in the dining rooms, while working through crab bisque and a generous portion of crab cocktail followed by a Chesapeake salad consisting of crab and rock shrimp handsomely garnished and accompanied by corn sticks, popovers and sweet butter. Another specialty of the inn is their Wye Island creation which consists of a properly prepared, thick crab cake layered into a toasted Kaiser roll. When weather permits, such fare should be taken on the inn's small porch, all the while watching the steady stream of residents and visitors rushing past.

Annapolis, its inner historic district core intact, has a great deal to attract the visitor, including fleets of commercial and pleasure craft of all sizes. The town is home to a good many yacht brokers and a not so small navy of noted sailors. For actual navy, there is the Academy with its gold cupola visible all over town, its tomb of John Paul Jones and its museum detailing the nation's naval history. Founded in 1845, the Naval Academy is the largest landowner in Annapolis. Old grads keep returning, as do sailors from everywhere, especially during the U.S. Sailboat Show in October—the largest in-the-water boat show in the world. Annapolis has become a major crossroads for old salts of all persuasions and the Annapolis Sailing School with its seven branches is the largest in the world. History buffs can look into all that landed history in the old Reynolds Tavern and at the Middleton Tavern on Market Place, where Washington and Jefferson were regulars.

MARYLAND INN, Church Circle, Annapolis, Maryland 21401. Telephone: (301) 2641. Accommodations: 44 rooms and suites; private baths; telephones; televisions. Rates: moderate. Full bar and meal service. Children permitted. Inquire about pets. Cards: AE, DC, MC, VISA. Open all year.

Getting There: The inn is on Church Circle, a block from the Capitol on State Circle.

GIBSON'S LODGINGS
Annapolis, Maryland

Less than a football field away from the City Dock of one of the most unremittingly picturesque harbors in the country are a pair of houses that have been painstakingly revitalized to serve as land-locked havens for any and all who come by car or boat. Responsible for the rebirth was a couple from Illinois who came to town a few years ago to indulge in their love of sailing. And in the sailing capital of the nation—if not the world, as they claim hereabouts—they decided to stay.

Sailors of all ages and tourists of all trades should be grateful. Located on Prince George Street close to all the waterborne action, they have converted an eighteenth-century property, which at one time was assigned to the Naval Officer of the Port of Annapolis, into a brick hideaway that would do justice to a far more expensive estate in Georgetown. Its interiors, along with its counterpart's, a later, nineteenth-century stucco two-story, are filled with various antiques (Annapolis has more than its fair share of antique-hunters and dealers), creating everywhere the sense of place and time. The innkeepers have achieved a praiseworthy model in adaptive restoration: retaining the old and adapting it to modern use.

The City Dock is the site of the annual Annapolis Arts Festival which started in 1962. In addition to the parade of arts and crafts, it features continual performances on the outdoor stage, including cloggers, rock groups, gymnasts and blue grass. The City Dock is also where one boards the *Harbor Queen*, a three hundred-passenger tour boat that cruises the harbor, the Severn River and the Chesapeake. The

twenty-two-passenger *Miss Anne* takes a fifty-minute tour along the waterfront and the one-hundred-passenger *Annapolitan II* spends a total of seven hours on the bay, stopping at St. Michaels and/or Oxford.

GIBSON'S LODGINGS, 110–114 Prince George Street, Annapolis, Maryland 21401. Telephone: (301) 268-5555. Accommodations: 14 rooms; seven with private baths; no telephones; no televisions. Rates: inexpensive, includes Continental breakfast. Children permitted. No pets. No cards. Open all year.

Getting There: Gibson's is about 75 yards from the city dock; from State Circle take East Street to Prince George and turn right, proceeding two blocks to the inn.

Brains, Bed and Board
OAKWOOD
Harwood, Maryland

Since 1981 the Brezinas, Joan and Dennis, have opened wide the doors of this delightful white frame country home. The Oakwood captures much of the spirit of the tidewater area, with its inviting yet hidden little hamlets, with its heritage that goes back to Captain John Smith. So near and yet so far from Washington, D.C.

Built a couple decades before the War Between the States by a family that like many in these parts, favored the Confederate cause, the Oakwood is really a rustic retreat, giving guests today the sense of living in the woods. There are wooded trails wandering off in several directions, some of which are organized by the Brezinas and lead past the old formal gardens, the foundations of the original stables and other outbuildings. In front, on a lawn shaded by giant trees, there are badminton and croquet courts.

The Brezinas restored Oakwood beautifully, bare-knuckling into the tasks of revitalization, scraping and painting, as well as carefully selecting the proper antiques to fit the small library to the right of the entrance and the dining room, where fresh-baked breads highlight the morning meal. Together they refinish furniture, and while Joan does needlepoint for relaxation, Dennis makes hook rugs. What better therapy for a Ph.D. economist from Yale and a graduate of Annapolis with an M.A. from Harvard?

The Brezinas represent a new breed of innkeeper: those who have not really stopped the world and tried to get off, but have courageously made a very special adjustment to it. In the process they have created a refuge close to the real worlds around—Washington to the west, Annapolis to the north and all those charming little tidewater towns to the south.

OAKWOOD, 4566 Solomons Island Road, Harwood, Maryland 20776. Telephone: (301) 261-5338. Accommodations: two rooms with shared bath; no telephones; no televisions. Rates: moderate, includes breakfast. No children or pets. No cards. Open all year.

Getting There: Follow State Road 2 twelve miles south to Harwood and then a dirt driveway to mailbox and sign, proceeding three-tenths of a mile to the inn.

A Rural Retreat
THE INN AT MITCHELL HOUSE
Chestertown, Maryland

Since the summer of 1982 this early eighteenth-century farmhouse, which was added to in 1825, has been a refreshingly rural retreat run by Al and Dorris Marshall. Knowledgeable collectors, the Marshalls have filled their six guest rooms with a very interesting collection of antiques. They also run the Antique Shoppe alongside the inn/farm house, which graces the old smokehouse.

The day at this inn begins as it should: with a let-it-all-hang-out, full-blown country breakfast—sometimes Southern style with grits, sometimes Pennsylvania Dutch style with scrapple, but always with freshly made muffins or other special breads. With that foundation, the guest is then prepared for a tour of the ten acres of surrounding inn land, alert for pheasants, migrating geese and swans, all kinds of song birds and maybe a white-tailed deer or two.

For more of the same, in a far larger arena, there is the Eastern Neck Island National Wildlife Refuge with opportunities for crabbing and clamming as well as for walking the nature trails. In town is the charm of Colonial Chestertown and to the south, in Centreville, more of the same—a flyer with a self-guided walking tour is available at the Queen Ann's County Courthouse, oldest in the state.

The inn will prepare a picnic basket for the day-trippers—they call it a Ploughman's Lunch. When you return, there is the sociability of the front parlour for discussing the day's activities, telling fish tales about the big ones that got away while casting lines in the bay or the Choptank River, or for planning where to go and what to do next.

Then there is the quiet of the guest rooms, each of them individually furnished and named after local figures of note, including Joseph T. Mitchell, who built this farmhouse in the middle of what used to be a thousand-acre holding. This room is really a minisuite, with a fireplace. Two of the other rooms have fireplaces, including the twin-bedded accommodation named Sir Peter Parker. He was the commander of British forces in the area during the War of 1812. Wounded at the battle at Caulk's Field, he was evacuated to the Mitchell House but could not be saved. His body was transported to his native England in a barrel of rum.

Maybe that is why there is no rum served at the inn; they do provide ice and setups for those who bring their own bottles. The Marshalls also provide lots of fresh flowers along with a generous portion of care and concern, and can discuss other stories of local lore and legend, advising on all there is to see and do in the area.

THE INN AT MITCHELL HOUSE, P.O. Box 329; R. D. 2, Tolchester Estates, Chestertown, Maryland 21620. Telephone: (301) 778-6500. Accommodations: six rooms and suites; three with private baths; no telephones; television in parlour. Rates: moderate, includes full breakfast and setups, complimentary beverage and fruit on arrival. Cards: MC, VISA. Small children not permitted. No pets. Open all year.

Getting There: Take State Road 20 from the center of Chestertown where the road commences at High Street and drive 7.7 miles to State Road 21; turn right and drive 2.7 miles to a dirt road and a small sign pointing the way to the inn—the turnoff is opposite an abandoned Nike site.

A Model Restoration

WHITE SWAN TAVERN

Chestertown, Maryland

Northernmost of the Chesapeake inns covered in this book, the White Swan represents the very best in the fine art of restoration. Incredible is not too strong a term to describe the achievement, the painstakingly perfect rebirth, which is detailed ever so professionally in a glassed-over portion of the wall and in exhibits showing the progress of revitalization, the archeological digs on the site, a group of before and after photos and some representative shards.

When Horace Havemeyer Jr., a man with an obvious passion for preservation of the past, bought the property in 1977, it was serving as a news agency. Before that it had been a music store and earlier, a shoe repair shop. Havemeyer and his researchers went back to the origins, identifying all the owners and residents and then memorializing their presence in various rooms. Thus, the ground floor guest room, with brick floor and original rafters overhead, a double and a twin bed and a private entrance from the yard, is known as the John Lovegrove Kitchen. It was put there by Lovegrove who was the town cobbler and had a tannery on the premises until he sold it in 1733.

Then there is the Joseph Nicholson Room, a smashing, successful re-creation of a public room. This eighteenth-century reincarnation honors the patriot who bought the home from Lovegrove and built a house in front of the original humble structure. Nicholson was a member of the all-important local Committee of Correspondence, influential in the founding of Washington College in town. He also kept an accurate inventory of his possessions and Havemeyer used it to refurnish the Nicholson Room. This room is now once again graced by a "Japaned Clock," as the patriot listed his grandfather clock with a lacquer-like design on the front panel.

During the dig, several chunks of highly polished black marble were unearthed and identified by the British Geological Museum as black fossil marble from County Kilkenny in Ireland. That was good enough for the restorers. There must have been such a marble fireplace in the tavern, so they imported another to put in its place. Another clever bit of detective work was done in identifying what type of cornices to put into first-floor rooms: in the attic they located pieces of the original woodwork, which had been removed in the late nineteenth century and used to reinforce the roof. That was during the time when the building was owned by Kent County's first millionaire, Thomas W. Eliason. Another notable owner was William N. Wilmer, one-time rector of Bruton Parish Church in Williamsburg, Virginia and president of William and Mary.

The history is all there, right down to Victorian times, and the suite furnished in that eclectic style is my favorite: the giant bed must cover at least half an acre. It's good to flop on after a day absorbing all there is to see and do in the charming Colonial town of Chestertown.

Founded in 1706, Chestertown is the seat of Kent County, chartered in 1632 by Lord Baltimore. In the Colonial Era it was an important port of entry for goods from the mother country and the many merchants who prospered from that trade built magnificent mansions along the Chester River.

Present-day owners have devoted considerable time and treasure to the task of restoring those memories and on the third Saturday of September there is an annual candlelight tour of many of the homes. They are easily identified by the walking tour map of the town available at the Kent County Chamber of Commerce, housed in a former school at 400 High Street. Close by is the Geddes-Piper House, at 101 Church Alley, open from 1:00 to 4:00 each Saturday. Restored by the Kent County Historical Society, it is now the headquarters of that organization, which can provide information on the homes along Water Street. Number 103 is the former Custom House and Number 106 is the home of the president of Chestertown's Washington College, a collection of Colonial brick buildings shaded by giant trees and framed by boxwood hedges. It's the tenth oldest college in the country, founded in 1782.

While walking on Water Street, detour a few hundred yards to the Old Wharf Inn on Cannon Street. Located on the muddy Chester, it is not quite as rugged inside as the name sounds or as it appears on the outside. A wall of windows looks out on the boat parade and the service is smiling. There are groaning table buffets and a superlative crab and clam bisque. Soft shells are also commendable.

WHITE SWAN TAVERN, 231 High Street, Chestertown, Maryland 21620. Telephone: (301) 776-2300. Accommodations: five rooms, private baths; no telephones; no televisions. Rates: expensive, includes Continental breakfast and setups. Children permitted. No pets. No cards. Open all year.

Getting There: Chestertown is in the northern neck of the Eastern Shore of Maryland on State Route 213, seventeen miles north of the intersection with U.S. 301. The inn is in the center of the town.

White Swan Tavern

Bigger Is Better

THE TIDEWATER INN
Easton, Maryland

It is definitely not a little old country inn and its origins do not go back many years. But there is such a super-abundance of Colonial charm and Federal design and so many modern amenities (including a Dow Jones ticker-tape)—and there is so much to do and see in the Easton vicinity—that The Tidewater simply must be put into a book of this sort.

Whether you check in with your camouflage clothes and start your day with the 5 a.m. Hunter's Bountiful Breakfast or come for a special budgetstretching weekend—working through the Friday night buffet and the Sunday morning brunch—you'll be pampered with a full parade of all the benefits of modern hotel keeping. There's an outdoor pool for summer use, nearby tennis and golf, shops and snackeries, the cleverly outfitted Decoy Bar, and as much updated Colonial charm as money and good taste allowed when it was built in 1949—and enlarged four years later. And Easton has the kind of historic homes and buildings that are a preservationist's dream.

The best place to start touring these dreams is a block from the Tidewater at the Historical Society of Talbot County. Located on South Washington Street, the Historical Society occupies the old Stevens House, built about 1800. The Society also oversees other properties, including a Federal-style garden, a Victorian store and an interesting collection of costumes and period furnishings, and they can organize walking tours of the town. The Society can also point out the location of the largest white oak tree in the U.S.: four centuries old, it is close to 100 feet tall and has a span of some 170 feet.

The Third Haven Friends Meeting House, three blocks south of the Historical Society on Washington Street, built in 1682 and enlarged a century later, is one of the oldest meeting houses in the country. Few other buildings survive from that early period of Quaker settlement, but there is a fine array of structures from later periods and the full range of American architecture can be quickly surveyed by walking along the town's streets. Across from the Tidewater Inn is the Talbot County Court House, dating from 1711, rebuilt in 1794 and remodeled several times after that—it used to be called the East Capitol of Maryland. Across the street is the Brick Hotel, built in 1812 and for years the leading hostelry on the Eastern Shore—it is now an office building. Next door is the 1803 Thomas Perrin Smith Home, headquarters for the Chesapeake Bay Yacht Club since 1912, and close by is the Bullitt House, one of Easton's oldest remaining homes, built in 1790 and now a real estate office.

THE TIDEWATER INN, Dover and Harrison Streets, Easton, Maryland 21601. Telephone: (301) 822-1300. Accommodations: 119 rooms and suites; private baths; telephones; televisions; AM/FM radios. Rates: expensive. Full bar and meal service. Children permitted. Inquire about pets. Cards: AE, CB, DC, MC, VISA. Open all year.

Getting There: The inn is on the corner of Dover and Harrison Streets in the center of town, which is less than a mile from U.S. 50 on State Road 331.

THE INN AT PERRY CABIN

St. Michaels, Maryland

The Navy purser who served under Commodore Oliver Hazard Perry during the War of 1812 had such great respect for his commander that he named his home in Perry's honor. Purser Samuel Hambleton built well, spreading his estate on the northern edge of a town that Britisher James Braddock had laid out in squares and lots in the 1770s. The focal point of that plan was and is St. Mary's Square, with its ship's carpenter's bell that has been rung daily since 1842 precisely at 7 a.m., noon and 5 p.m.

The bell marked the working day for the many carpenters who worked at local shipyards in this very nautical town, one with not only an inn named for one of our most famous naval heroes, but also with a marvelous Chesapeake Bay Maritime Museum. The museum is stretched across sixteen acres of buildings old and new on a peninsula in the harbor. The work of those ships' carpenters is shown in abundance, in the old log-bottom bugeye and racing canoe, in the skipjack and all kinds of pleasure craft. There is also a wonderful collection of decoys and displays brilliantly showing the extensive wild waterfowl population of the St. Michaels area.

St. Michaels was a target of the British fleet in the War of 1812 because of the shipbuilding activity—the famed Baltimore Clippers were sawn and hammered together here—and in town is a reminder of the bombardments which occasionally hit other structures. On St. Mary's Square is the Cannonball House where, as local lore has it, a British missile came roaring through the roof and bounced down the stairs. terrorizing the wife of the shipwright who had built it, William Merchant.

Another shipbuilder, Wrightson Jones, had yards at Beverly on San Domingo Creek and built his home just off the square on the corner of Mulberry and Talbot Streets in 1816. He put in a cellar, an uncommon extra in the low-lying town. Shipwright Robert Lambdin's cottage, built of hickory, mortised and pegged, is closer to the harbor. This style of construction, in which all joints are mortised and tenoned with wooden pegs, is also seen at the St. Mary's Square Museum, across the green from the Cannonball House. It is built of half timbers cut and shaped with a broad ax, and it has been carefully restored and beautifully furnished in loyalty to its Colonial beginnings. The Museum also publishes a self-guided walking tour brochure, which is a necessary aid, for very few of the historic buildings are open to the public or have identifying sings.

But the Inn at Perry Cabin is hard to miss. The inn is shaded by giant trees, immaculately landscaped and manicured, and has a happy little gazebo of a bar on the lawn and water all around—guests can arrive by boat as well as by car. It also sports a surprise of a bar, one named for Spectacular Bid, champion throughbred in the stable of innkeeper Ron Thomas. Appropriately enough, this bar with all its racing memorabilia was built into the former carriage house of the estate.

Neither Commodore Perry nor his purser would recognize the place today with its trio of dining rooms (all overlooking the Miles River) that bar and all the modern conveniences. However, when the Meyerhoffs revitalized the historic home, they took great pains to preserve as much of the past as was practicable: moldings and mantels, door frames, and that magnificent swirl of a stairway leading to the second floor guestrooms. They too respect the past and are carefully color-coordinated and handsomely executed, thanks to the efforts of decorator Anthony Bromley whose shop is in Easton, on Harrison Street. Of the half dozen rooms, a favorite is Number 20, with its rich green trim, the Audubon print which picks up the browns and beiges of the fabrics, and the covered headboard which lends a rather regal touch.

THE INN AT PERRY CABIN, Talbot Street (P.O. Box 247), St. Michaels, Maryland 21663. Telephone: (301) 745-5178. Accommodations: six rooms; private baths; telephones; no televisions. Rates: expensive, includes Continental breakfast. Full bar and meal service. Children permitted. Inquire about pets. Cards: AE, MC, VISA. Open all year.

Getting There: The inn is at the northern edge of town next to the baseball field; the town is nine miles west of Easton on State Road 33.

Nothing Unkempt at tne Kemp
KEMP HOUSE INN
St. Michaels, Maryland

In 1805 local shipyard owner Joseph Kemp built this prim and proper-looking three-story Georgian home not far from San Domingo Creek. Seven years later he was named Colonel, in charge of the town militia defending against the bombarding British. His solidly built home today serves as an in-town inn, a carefully kept step into the past, filled with handmade furnishings arrayed and assembled in a manner suggesting the simplicity of the Shakers.

"Publick Lodging" the sign reads by the orderly little white rail fence, inviting the guest into an earlier time, one with four-poster rope beds, bursts of fresh flowers, fireplaces, candles and whale oil lamps. There are thick quilts for chilly evenings, trundle beds for the wee ones, and everywhere a great sense of cozy comfort of a century or two ago. And breakfast in bed for those who so desire—the mornings's delivery brings cheeses and fresh fruit and something in pastry reminiscent of Pennsylvania Dutch country—but why not? The owners also own an inn in that part of the world, an inn of the same name in Ephrata, described elsewhere in this book.

Across the street from the inn is the Bruff House, a Colonial Southern Marine-style home with so-called cross doors, each with a cross on the front but which are plain on the back. Across the other street, Talbot, the one-time Main Street, is Dr. Miller's Farmhouse, a brick home as solidly built as Smithton but put up thirty-five years later. A block away is Mount Pleasant, across from the post office and dating from 1806, and The Old Inn, which dates from 1816.

In addition to land-bound tours of St. Michaels, there is the ferry which crosses the Tred Avon River to Oxford, and the ninety-minute cruises along the Miles River on the *Patriot,* a one-hundred-passenger boat which makes three trips daily from June through September (and in winter months takes popular luncheon cruises in Florida, from Boynton Beach to Pal's Captain's Table in Deerfield Beach).

KEMP HOUSE INN, 412 South Talbot Street (P.O. Box 638), St. Michaels, Maryland 21663. Telephone: (301) 745-5793. Accommodations: six rooms; two share bath, all share shower rooms; no telephones; no television. Rates: inexpensive to moderate, includes Continental breakfast. Children permitted. No pets. Cards: MC, VISA. Open all year.

Family Budget Pleaser
THE PASADENA
Royal Oak, Maryland

"Wunderbar by the Sea" is the way this 22-year-old plantation mansion is billed by owners Schwaben International, a worldwide organization dedicated to "better world understanding." They sponsor various conferences and seminars in the white rambling giant, one that grew, from all external appearances, like Topsy: there is an added-on wraparound porch, a front entry Greek Revival portico, various shelters and outbuildings and a quartet of cottages across the road from the main building, which has forty-four rooms for guests.

The Pasadena is anything but formal. Or expensive. It is really a family compound, one in which all ages can find something to do on the 135 acres: swimming in the pool, waterskiing, playing shuffleboard or croquet or heading out into the bay for boating or fishing, or helping the staff harvest the fresh-grown vegetables in their own farm patches. One can wander around the grounds which are as naturally and informally kept as the accommodations, sit under an ancient magnolia or linden tree and listen to the sounds of nature and the songs of the birds, or take expeditions into the charming towns of Oxford and St. Michaels.

The meals are simple but solid and there is a great sense of camaraderie among the people who discover the Pasadena. When I first came upon the monstrous white ghost in the woods, there was a group of watercolorists there for a workshop. A few days earlier, a contingent from Bloomie's had arrived, taking the four-hour bus ride from New York in order to spend a day to unbend, unwind, un-whatever before returning to the grind. And they did not have to check with their bankers before signing up for the excursion. The Pasadena is as inexpensive as it is informal.

THE PASADENA, Route 329 (P.O. Box 187), Royal Oak, Maryland 21662. Telephone: (301) 745-5053. Accommodations: 35 rooms, 18 with private baths; four cottages with private baths; no telephones; television in common room. Rates: inexpensive to moderate. Full bar and meal service. Children permitted. Inquire about pets. Cards: MC, VISA. Open end of March until late November.

Getting There: Royal Oak is on State Road 329, one mile south of State Road 33 which runs between Easton and St. Michaels.

HARRISON'S CHESAPEAKE HOUSE
Tilghman Island, Maryland

Tilghman Island, north of the Choptank River and reached by a drawbridge over Knapps Narrows, is named for Revolutionary War hero Tench Tilghman, the Lt. Colonel who carried the message of Cornwallis's surrender from Yorktown to the Continental Congress in Philadelphia. Born on Old Villa Road near Easton (a stone marker is on the spot) and buried in the Oxford Cemetery where there is a monument marking the grave, Tilghman was friend and aide-de-camp to Washington. The stretch of land which bears his name today is the headquarters of the Talbot County seafood industry—a ten million dollar industry—and everywhere the visitor today sees boats of all shapes and sizes, many of them available for charter.

One of the largest charter fleets is that under the captaincy of Buddy Harrison, whose family also runs the Chesapeake House. A fisherman's delight, with special "Buddy Plan" packages including room, all meals, boat and tackle, the Harrisons will even clean and pack your catch—for a slight extra charge. In fact, Buddy's twelve boats make him, he claims, the "largest charter fleet on the Bay." And if a group arrives by bus and numbers thirty or more, Buddy will organize a free boat ride with lunch or dinner.

These meals feature a harvest of the deep, honestly prepared and served in a classic fish house, water-hugging setting. Meals here should start with backfin crabmeat cocktail, cream of crab or Maryland crab soup, and then comes an Eastern Shore Dinner. That spells crab cakes and fried chicken delivered with a garden-fresh variety of vegetables and homemade bread, climaxed by baked-out-back pie.

The dining room at the Chesapeake also sautées its lump crabmeat and serves it, as they do their soft shell crabs, with sliced ham. They give shrimp the scampi, garlic butter and french fry treatment as well as stuffing them with more crabmeat, and they prepare superlative scallops: broiling, frying, or best, baking them in a deliciously tangy cheese concoction.

The oldest portion of the inn was built in 1856 and the rooms there are slightly less expensive than in the newer motel-style addition, but I like any of the rooms—simply furnished in a functional manner but very well-maintained—which have a view of the action on the water. And then I like to sit on the front porch overlooking not the bay, but the well-trimmed garden, conversing with all the friendly people on the staff and those fisher folk who come back to the Chesapeake year after year.

HARRISON'S CHESAPEAKE HOUSE, Tighman Island, Maryland 21671. Telephone: (301) 886-2121. Accommodations: 60 rooms: 50 with private baths; no telephones; no televisions. Rates: inexpensive. Full bar and meal service. Children permitted. No pets. Cards: AE, MC, VISA. Open April 15 through November 30.

Getting There: Follow State Road 33 into the town of Tilghman and to the large white two-story double-porched building on the left side of the road.

Come by Land or Water

TILGHMAN INN

Tilghman Island, Maryland

Where the Choptank River meets Chesapeake Bay at Knapps Narrows, is this new, immaculately maintained, ultra-modern hostelry with a grand view of the water. It has its own dock for those who arrive by boat and a setting that is so nautical they even put crushed oyster shell into the beds of shrubbery.

The rooms are clean and modern with brass beds and, for those who arrive by boat, there are eleven slips at dockside (the eastern end of Knapps Narrows) with gas and diesel, ice, and cold beer. What more could a boat want? And what more its passengers than the Friday night seafood specials in the dining room, the Thursday night prime rib or the Sunday brunch with all kinds of homemade desserts?

For those who want to spend a weekend or longer trying their luck hooking the denizens of the deep, there are special package arrangements—the inn arranges for charter boats for parties of six or more. But if you're only one, two or three, not to worry, says the Tilghman Inn: they will make up the party.

And on weekends they will also provide movies and live entertainment in the lounge for the amusement of their guests after dinner. The Tilghman Inn provides feasts of freshly steamed crabs Maryland style (and that means a shower of Old Bay seasoning) or an array of meats plucked off the outdoor barbecue pit. For those who bring their own— fish or some feathered fowl during the hunting season—the kitchen will prepare the catch. It will then be served in a spring-bright dining room by a smiling staff that is convinced they have the best seafood menu in the state.

In the proper season, May through October, the Yacht's View Deck is the perfect place to while away a few hours in the open air, watching the commercial crabbers and oystermen, planning to tour one of the packing plants where the harvest from the briny blue is processed for shipping all across the land. Crabbing parties can be organized as well as fishing charters, and the inn also has a crab farm where one can watch the soft shells get cleaned and packed—or they can be purchased live.

TILGHMAN INN, Coopertown Road, Tilghman Island, Maryland 21671. Telephone: (301) 886-2141. Accommodations: 20 rooms; private baths; no telephones; no televisions. Rates: inexpensive. Full bar service; lunch and dinner daily April 15 through November 30, remainder of year Thursday through Sunday. Children permitted. Inquire about pets. Cards: AE, MC, VISA. Open all year.

Getting There: The inn is on the island end of the bridge on State Road 33 leading into town; it overlooks Knapps Narrows.

The Inn of Inns
ROBERT MORRIS INN
Oxford, Maryland

Of the innumerable inns I have visited all over this land and abroad, the Robert Morris, in the close-to-unbelieveable, time-stood-still setting of Oxford, comes very close to qualifying as the *ne plus ultra.* Heavy with history, surrounded by perfectly preserved homes, providing a variety of comfortable accommodations and superior food, the Robert Morris Inn is one of those places you want to return to—again and again.

The oldest part of the inn with its splendid staircase dates from the earliest years of the eighteenth century, when beams were hand-hewn, the paneling was put in place with wooden pegs, and oversize ship nails were used in construction. In 1730 Robert Morris moved in. The English representative of a large London shipping and trading company, he was assigned to this all-important port, which was founded before Baltimore and shared, with the town of Annapolis, the position of leading port of entry on the Chesapeake.

The ferry service from those days, which crossed the Tred Avon River a few feet from the inn and connected Oxford with Bellevue, is still in existence and is the oldest ferry of the non-cable variety in continuous service in the country. It has been carrying passengers, goods and vehicles since 1760, when the fare was paid in tobacco. Other highlights of local history are related in the small Oxford Town Museum next door to the Town Hall, not far from the so-called Grapevine House with the largest vine I've seen outside a Tarzan movie—it was brought to Oxford from the Isle of Jersey in 1810.

And there's history in abundance in the inn—the walls talk. Of Robert Morris the successful businessman who died in a freak accident in 1750: he was struck by the wadding from a ship's gun being fired in his honor and is buried in the graveyard near the ruins of the White Marsh Church in Easton. Robert Morris Jr., his son, gained fame as the "Financier of the Revolution." When few had the courage or the cash to risk fame and fortune on the radicals preaching independence, Morris staked his friend, George Washington, using all his savings to support the fledgling Continental Army, and then served as Financial Agent of the Marine Department.

The inn that bears his name and that of his father does honor to both. Innkeepers Wendy and Ken Gibson work tirelessly to match the challenge of all that history, striving mightily to present a dining room that alone is worth the trip, history or no. The setting is marvelous: the murals were created from wallpaper samples used by manufacturers' reps a century and a half ago; the slate floor in the tavern came from Vermont; the chimney was inspired by the one in the Raleigh Tavern in Williamsburg; there is a fine carving of the Morris coat of arms; and a hand-carved log canoe under sail.

Start an evening at the inn with a Seventeen Ten, a rum-fruit concoction served in a take-home crested colonial squall glass, then order the oysters à la Gino, a sensibly-spiced, crabmeat-filled, broiled-with-bacon delight that will get all the juices flowing. Or on colder evenings when the fireplaces are crackling their merry welcome, have a hot buttered rum and some of the superior crab soup which, along with crab cakes and crab imperial, is a house specialty. The salad dressings are freshly made and are marvelous, including the low-cal offering; the fisherman's salad bowl for lunch is equally fresh and most generous in portion. Lunch is taken in the Tap Room with its heavy timbers and dark woods, its polished tables and all kinds of nautical art on the walls and thick, wide planks on the floor.

There is more wide planking in the guest rooms in the original part of Morris's home, along with pegged paneling and fireplaces made from brick brought over from the mother country as ballast.

ROBERT MORRIS INN, on the Tred Avon (P.O. Box 70), Oxford, Maryland 21654. Telephone: (301) 226-5111. Accommodations: 30 rooms, cottage, river house, lodge and apartment; most with private baths; no telephones, no television. Rates: inexpensive to expensive. Full bar and meal service. No children. No pets. Cards: AE, MC, VISA. Closed mid January–mid March.

Getting There: The inn is at water's edge at the end of State Road 333 in Oxford.

Historic Mansion
NANTICOKE MANOR HOUSE
Vienna, Maryland

Nanticoke is another one of those marvelously mysterious Indian words—like Choptank and Pocomoke, Wicomico and Chicamaconico—that dot Chesapeake Bay maps with such individuality. Nanticoke is the name of the river which winds south to the bay from such feeder streams as Trussum Pond and Marshyhope Creek. It was first explored by Captain John Smith in 1608, and a century later its chief settlement was chartered by the Colonial Assembly as the town of Vienna, named after the Austrian city or perhaps for a local Indian leader named Vinnacokasimmon.

Nanticoke Manor was the name given to the ten-thousand-acre tract along the northern shore of the river patented in 1664 and granted to Lord Baltimore. And Nanticoke Manor was the name selected by the innkeepers who restored the distinctive structure and decided to share it with guests who want to immerse themselves totally in the history of this Dorchester County slice of somnolence.

Built in 1861, the Federal box of a Victorian is probably the result of additions to an earlier, far more modest dwelling from the previous century. Known locally as The Brick House, it was the first in town to be made from bricks. Its first owner, James K. Lewis, was obviously a man of substance, a ship's captain and merchant, for he constructed an impressive dwelling with high ceilings, molded cornices, plaster medallions, a wealth of windows, wooden paneling and a magnificent sweeping three-story spiral staircase.

Furnishings in the guestrooms, the parlour and the dining room have been selected with a careful eye to the prosperous past of the

153

mansion. There is a partially screened front porch which is ideal for watching the nonaction of this old Indian settlement that used to be known as Emperor's landing or exchanging stories about local sight-seeing.

A self-guided walking tour flyer is available at the inn which will guide the guest to other historic homes. Next door to the Manor House, sitting alongside the banks of the river, is The Customs House, dating from 1768, the year when Vienna was declared area customs district. A few yards on the other side of the Manor House is the Old Methodist Episcopal Church and Cemetary; the Collins Cottage from the early years of the nineteenth century; the Percy Lecompte House, a couple of decades older; and the Bratten House of the same vintage. Across the street from the latter is the magnificent Thomas Higgins House, built about 1870 and laden with gingerbread trim in the best Victorian manner. Across Church Street from the inn is the Thomas Holliday Hicks Home, which was constructed in the first years of the new nation and was home to the man who later became governor for eleven years. Holliday was in office during the early part of the Civil War and fought vigorously against the will of those state legislators who wanted to bring Maryland into the Confederate cause. None of these houses is open to the public, but during the annual Vienna Heritage Celebration, the second or third Saturday of May, and the Vienna Candlelight Tour, the second or third Saturday of December, some of them might open their doors.

A historic structure that, like the Nanticoke Manor House, is open to the public is The Tavern House, a working inn since Colonial days—the proprietor usually had a monopoly on the Nanticoke River ferry. Today it serves as town tavern, a Colonial escape with crackling fireplaces, masses of mortised carpentry and a happy atmosphere.

Other buildings of interest in the area—there are so many they have been grouped together into a Historic District—can be found about half way between Vienna and Cambridge, in East Newmarket on State Road 16 as well as in nearby Secretary, proud of its 1662 My Lady Sewall's Manor.

NANTICOKE MANOR HOUSE, Church Street (P.O. Box 156), Vienna, Maryland 21869. Telephone: (301) 376-3530. Accommodations: five rooms; two with private baths; one efficiency apartment with private bath; telephones; no televisions. Rates: moderate, includes Continental breakfast (or full breakfast if ordered in advance). Children permitted. No pets. No cards. Open March through December.

Getting There: Coming from Cambridge on U.S. 50, turn right at the only traffic light in Vienna; at stop sign turn left on Race Street. At the river, turn right on Water Street and drive two-tenths of a mile to the inn on Church Street (also known as Broad Street).

Old in Years, Modern in Comfort
WASHINGTON HOTEL
Princess Anne, Maryland

King George II was on the throne when this hotel was opened in his North American colony in 1744, two years after the town became the county seat. A prominent citizen of the time was Samuel Chase, who thirty years later signed the Declaration of Independence to break away from George II's successor, and today there are several buildings surviving from those Colonial days. Namely, the Tunstall Cottage on the corner of Broad and Church Streets, built as a one and one-half story frame cottage in 1705 and still occupied today. At the other end of the block, on the corner of Church and Prince William Streets, is the 1750 Karol House with its Victorian addition, surrounded by many other homes that were built in the Victorian era. However, the Federal style does survive, especially in the clump of buildings at Broad and Somerset, as well as in the Fitzgerald House and the McGruder and the Carey homes on Prince William and Nansion Streets.

The Teackle Mansion from 1802 is the most interesting Federal-style leftover. Built of brick with a gabled central block and patterned after a Scottish manor, the mansion now serves as a museum, open only on Sundays or by appointment. It contains an interesting assemblage of costumes and decorative arts and a collection of documents and prints illustrating the history of Princess Anne and Somerset County. They, or the county's Tourist Center (telephone (301) 651-2968), will be able to advise the dates of Olde Princess Anne Days, when many of the private homes are open to the public.

But the Washington Hotel is always open. It has been under the direction of Mrs. Mary A. Murphey ever since 1947 when she took over for her husband who ran the landmark where some say George actually did spend the night. Others deny that story, as they deny many of the other stories circulating about the history of the hostelry with its collection of antiques and curiosities. On one wall are prints or photographs of all the presidents and on another their first ladies.

Washington Hotel

The setting is a curious counterpoint to the modernity of the guest rooms on the second floor or the non-Colonial setting of the dining room, which is in the capable hands of Mary's son, Robert. The fare there is simple and as straightforward as those chairs on the sheltered front porch—perfect for watching the nonaction in this sleepy little settlement of some seven hundred souls.

WASHINGTON HOTEL, Somerset Avenue, Princess Anne, Maryland 21853. Telephone: (301) 651-2525. Accommodations: 12 rooms; private baths; no telephones; cable television. Rates: inexpensive. Full bar and meal service. Children permitted. No pets. Cards: MC, VISA. Open all year.

Getting There: The hotel is in the center of town on Somerset Avenue, which runs parallel to State Road 13 which leads into town.

SMITH ISLAND

What Tangier is to Virginia, Smith Island is to Maryland: part of a chain of low-flying, marshy outcroppings of land, its sole inhabited off-shore island is reachable only by boat.

That boat is *Island Belle II,* successor to *Island Belle I* which ran from 1916 to 1977. It departs on a regular schedule from the city dock at Crisfield, located at the end of the line—the termination of State Road 413. It departs for Smith Island at Ewell daily at 12:30 p.m. making the fourteen-mile return trip at 4 p.m., leaving again for Ewell at 5 p.m. and departing from there 8 a.m. the following day.

Ewell is where the Pitchcroft Restaurant is located, the destination of most of the summertime tourists who like the short trip on the water and the home cooking and serving in a farmhouse that was built during the Revolutionary War. There are all kinds of freshly assembled sandwiches and freshly brewed soups, sizzling steaks, steamed crabs (ordered in advance) and soft shells.

Seafood is, of course, the specialty and it is guaranteed to be right out of the water. Seafood is how the Smith Islanders at Ewell support themselves and has been ever since the earliest times, when the first fishermen were outlaws and bandits hiding from the authorities. But those who live by the sea today are God-fearing, law-abiding souls who support the island's Methodist Church vigorously and sincerely, as they do on Virginia's Tangier Island.

Their lifestyle, their homes (many of them a couple of centuries old), their rugged simplicity and sense of isolation, and above all their language—which sounds as though they've recently stepped off the boat from Cornwall and English Lake Country—can easily be studied by someone interested in remaining for more than a meal however.

And there are several homes which take overnight guests, all of them operating at inexpensive levels and at prices which include full dinners and breakfasts. They all have a Ewell, Maryland 21824 address and are as follows: Pitchcroft (301/425-5851) has four units and can make arrangements for weekly rentals of Barbara's Tourist Home (301/425-5431), which has three bedrooms, bath and kitchen.

Mrs. Bernice Guy's (301/425-2751) has two rooms for guests, one with twin beds and one with a double, sharing baths, as do other accommodations.

Frances Kitching's (301/425-3321) has five units and she's the lady who wrote the island cookbook.

The Smith Island season runs from April 1 to November 1 and the visitor planning an overnight should not expect the Hilton or even a Days Inn. But they should expect a concern for comfort, a return to a simpler time, and mountains of honestly prepared seafood and down home specialties.

DELAWARE

Not the smallest of the fifty—despite those detractors who insist on saying "Dela-where?"—but it is most certainly the first of the fifty, a bantam-sized state that was the first to ratify the Constitution and thus the first to be admitted to the newly formed nation. It has no inferiority complexes about its size. In fact, the predominantly rural stretch of fertility, which is less than one hundred miles long and never wider than thirty-five is proud of the fact that its population just barely tops six hundred thousand (smaller than Dallas or Detroit). And their lawyers are certainly proud that more than half the Fortune 500 and over a third of all companies listed on the New York Stock Exchange are incorporated in Delaware, including of course the giant Du Pont firm, whose name is practically synonomous with the First State.

The du Pont presence is everywhere felt: in the Wilmington board rooms; in the state house and governor's mansion in the capital of Dover, in the chemical complex of the northern counties above the Chesapeake and Delaware Canal; and in the elegant estates of the Brandywine Valley, especially the 515-acre Granogue of the early 1920s and Winterthur. Grandest of them all, Winterthur was converted from a 196-room private mansion to a public museum by the beneficience of Henry Francis du Pont in 1951.

Winterthur is indeed the "Collection of Collections," the world's largest assemblage of American decorative arts with over fifty thousand objects made or used in this country between 1640 and 1840. But it is also a 963-acre research and learning center with a botanist's dream of a garden; with graduate programs for University of Delaware students; with its own publishing projects and art conservation programs; and with a group of historic buildings under its protective wing open to the public in Odessa. There is the 1774 Corbit-Sharp House in high Georgian style, the earlier and less elaborate Wilson-Warner House and the Federal-style 1822 Brick Hotel, now filled with a fine collection of American paintings, furniture and silver.

On the first Sunday of May is the annual Winterthur Point-to-Point Race, and the Winterthur Country Fair is held on the last sunday in September. These events attract thousands of spectators and are held on the spectacular grounds of the estate.

Not far from Winterthur is Nemours, the three hundred-acre estate named by its builder, Alfred I. du Pont, after the site of the du Pont ancestral home in the north of France. An American interpretation of a Louis XVI chateau, it was designed by the same Carrere and Hastings partnership responsible for numerous other monumental structures in the pre-World War I period. Among them are the Palm Beach mansion built for Florida's premier developer, Henry Morrison Flagler, the Metropolitan Opera House; the Congressional Office Building; and the New York Public Library.

A few miles north of Winterthur is the Hillendale Museum, a delight of dioramas detailing the westward movement across the continent, and the Brandywine River Museum, a converted nineteenth-century gristmill filled with the works of Maxfield Parrish (the dean of American illustrators), Howard Pyle, and three generations of Wyeths— Andrew's, of course, but also Father Wyeth's splendid illustrations for the works of Robert Louis Stevenson, and son Jamie, with his famous *Pig*. Just across the border in Pennsylvania are the Longwood Gardens, among the world's best, with illuminated fountains and all kinds of special events and observances.

South of Winterthur are the Delaware Museum of Natural History; the Art Museum with the largest collection of pre-Raphaelite painting in the country and masterworks by Howard Pyle; and the Hagley Museum, set on two hundred acres alongside the Brandywine River, the site of Du Pont's first black powder mill and of an early eighteenth-century Georgian residence that housed five generations of Du Ponts.

South of the Hagley Museum is the state's largest city, Wilmington, an important port with vibrant memories of its distant past, with memorials to that eleventh day of February, 1638, when the ship *Kalmar Nyckel* brought a hardy band of Swedish and Finnish colonists to the New World. The fort they quickly constructed, Christina, was named for their Swedish queen, as was the river which refreshed them. They were the colony of New Sweden, destined to survive just seventeen years. But before being subdued by Peter Stuyvesant, they managed to erect the first log cabins in this country. An early survivor of that great gift to America, one with rough-hewn logs saddle-notched and chinked with clay and tangled with twigs and grass, has been preserved and stands today rather forlornly in Wilmington's Fort Christina State Park. Close to it is a monument by famed Swedish sculptor Carl Milles marking the landing site of the Swedes, and Old Swedes Church, now known as Holy Trinity. Built in 1698, it is the oldest church still standing in the U.S. that has been regularly used for religious services.

The restored and relocated early home of Wilmington's Willmington Square, one of which now houses the Visitors Bureau, include the grand old 1871 Opera House, built of cast iron and brilliantly reborn as the Delaware Center for the Performing Arts. Gracing one side of nearby Rodney Square is the Hotel Du Pont, constructed during World War I and still as elegant as ever. It provides the kind of special experience sought when searching out the other hostelries in this book. Its Brandywine Restaurant boasts, among other works of art, three canvases by the three Wyeths. For information and reservations telephone (800) 323-7500.

The Inn That Was In Before Inns Were In

THE CORNER CUPBOARD INN
Rehoboth Beach, Delaware

Tucked into a thicket of trees and surrounded by grand echoes of the past in Rehoboth Beach's residential Pines section, the Corner Cupboard is deceptive from the road, from the narrow lane of sand winding under the pine and through the holly. Where do they manage to put fourteen rooms? Under a three-story, peaked roof which was at one time a private home, built in the late 1920s. Ask innkeeper Elizabeth Gundry Hooper and she'll gladly give you the tour, explaining about the antiques in the rooms, about the solarium, which in wintertime is an indoor garden and a rallying point for guests who like the warmth of the Franklin stove.

Summertime, visitors on their way to the beach one and one-half blocks away or to other activities, have their breakfasts in the early morning sunshine, digging into eggs and home fries, scrapple, sausage and sometimes kidney stew. There is a cheerful brick fireplace in the living room, a magnet for wintertime guests. It leads into the dining room which bustles during the high season—Memorial Day through mid-September—when it is open to the public for breakfast, dinner and Sunday brunch.

In season, the kitchen sends out appetite-stimulating scents and sniffs all day long. The menu varies but there are always freshly baked breads and pies, and seafood is a specialty. Meals start with a thick bisque of clam, crabmeat or shrimp cocktails, and proceed to a fresh fish of the day, lobster, crab imperial or a serving of soft shells— trapped in the nearby Chesapeake. Landlocked palates are not ignored in the pleasantly illuminated dining room with its fine flatware and Wedgewood: onion-smothered liver, prime rib, duckling, and sweetbreads freckled with chunks of ham are also on the bill of fare.

A favorite retreat after pushing myself away from this feasting is the trio of rooms in the back of the Corner Cupboard featuring a four-poster and overlooking the pleasant little brick courtyard. No room is uncomfortable, however, and there is a warm at-home feeling; it's a happy place to return to after a day at the beach or a day spent on the road exploring the area. Unlike Maryland's Ocean City, which seems to have totally succumbed to High Tack, Rehoboth Beach is much more than seashore eyesores.

Mrs. Hooper, innkeeper since 1971 and who before that worked for the owners, her aunt and uncle, can steer the guest to the many interesting attractions. On Martin's Lawn is the Anna Hazard Museum, Rehoboth Beach's first and only museum, open on weekends during the season. It provides some insights into the town's origins as a Methodist camp meeting.

In Lewes (pronounced Lew-is), seven miles distant at the head of Delaware Bay, there is a replica of the City Hall in Hoorn, Holland, built in 1931 on the three hundredth anniversary of the first European settlement in Delaware. The Dutch called their new town Zwaanendael,

but it was soon only a memory, for they were massacred by the Indians within a year. Later Dutch arrivals included Cornelius Plockhoy, who established the first Mennonite colony in this country—at Lewes, then known for some odd reason as Whorekill.

Other worthwhile structures in the Lewes Historic District, many of them strictly Victorian, include a small marine museum, an old country store and a blacksmith shop. At the eastern end of town is the Cape May–Lewes ferry which year-round chugs across the sixteen miles of Delaware Bay. In seventy minutes, this ferry takes the traveler (by foot or car) to the Jersey shore and one of the most intensely Victorian memory banks to be found anywhere in the country.

Between Lewes and Reheboth Beach is Cape Henlopen State Park, one thousand acres set aside where the ocean meets the bay. Here there are the famous "walking" sand dunes and all kinds of opportunities for surf fishing, swimming and for guided walks along nature trails. Crabbers and clammers congregate farther south near Rehoboth Bay, the Rehoboth Beach Canal and Love Creek. First-timers at that sport are advised to check with local bait and tackle stores; they can also advise the angler about deep-sea charters.

THE CORNER CUPBOARD INN, 50 Park Avenue, Rehoboth Beach, Delaware 19971. Telephone: (302) 227-8553. Accommodations: 18 rooms; all with private baths; no telephones; television in the solarium. Rates: moderate. Breakfast served year-round; dinner Memorial Day to mid-September; set-ups provided. Children permitted. Pets permitted in some rooms for a nominal charge; inquire first. Cards: AE, MC, VISA. Open all year except major holidays.

Getting There: From the main street, Rehoboth Avenue, turn left at the lighthouse onto Columbia Avenue and turn right on Second Street; drive one block to Park Avenue; turn left to reach the inn.

You'll Get a Glad Hand at the Gladstone
GLADSTONE INN
Rehoboth Beach, Delaware

There's a wonderful and warm, small town-homey American look and feel about the Gladstone—it's not nearly as pretentious as the name. A three-story eggshell-white frame with inviting green shutters, the Gladstone is fronted by a carefully trimmed lawn with clumps of green and bursts of bright flowers framing the full-length front porch. An American flag waves proudly in front of the rockers and yacht chairs positioned for lazy summer days and balmy nights, perfect for watching the residents of this vintage beachfront spread of modest homes and cottages, spruce up their property. Another plus: the inn is only two doors from the beach and three blocks from town.

A classic Victorian cottage dating from the early years of the century, the Gladstone is now in the able hands of Emma Mills, who operates the inn only during the summer season. In harsher months she lives in Smyrna, north of the capital city, Dover, itself a worthwhile destination for all those interested in the many manifestations of Victoriana. There are close to half a thousand buildings in the Smyrna Historic District. Some of the more fascinating are open to the public each year during the "Autumn in Duck Creek" celebration, held the third Saturday in October.

GLADSTONE INN, 3 Olive Avenue, Rehoboth Beach, Delaware 19971. Telephone: (302) 227-2641. Winter address: 119 Commerce Street, Smyrna, Delaware 19977. Telephone: (301) 653-8294. Accommodations: six rooms with shared baths; four apartments with private baths; no telephone; television in the living room. Rates: inexpensive. Children permitted. No pets. No cards. Open May 15–October 1.

Getting There: On Rehoboth Avenue drive toward the ocean and a block from the water turn left on First Street; drive three blocks to Olive and turn right.

Gladstone Inn

An Inn That Says Its Own Name

THE PLEASANT INN
Rehoboth Beach, Delaware

This inn not only defines its own name, it also defines the name of its owner-operator. Peck Pleasanton is a hospitable sort who runs a real estate business out of his inn and seems to know everyone in town. Bounding around the sweeping front porch, advising guests where to eat in town, on what to see in the area as well as what to avoid, and explaining the second floor coffee bar and the "Scouts Honor" wet bar in the corner of the giant porch with its panoramas of streets and sea— Peck is a dynamo.

Handsomely positioned in a grove of trees a few hundred meters from the sea and the Gladstone Inn, this most pleasant place has a real country inn look and is anything but a seaside cottage. It was moved to its present site after the great storm which swept these shores in 1918, and was converted from a home to an inn a decade later. That is when the single-bedroom carriage house on the grounds, with its fine little glassed-in patio, was also transformed to hostelry.

THE PLEASANT INN, 31 Olive Avenue, Rehoboth Beach, Delaware 19971. Telephone: (302) 227-7311. Accommodations: 10 rooms; private baths; no telephones; no televisions; two apartment units with private baths and entrances, fully-equipped kitchens; one carriage house (guests provide linens; telephone and television cable hookup billed separately). Rates: moderate. Children not permitted. Cards: MC, VISA. Open all year.

166

Getting There: From Rehoboth Avenue driving toward the ocean, turn left on First Street a block from the water and drive three blocks to Olive; the inn is on the corner.

By the Sea, By the Sea, By the Beautiful Sea

SEA LODGE
Rehoboth Beach, Delaware

Beachgoers wishing to stretch their budgets without sacrificing friendly attention by innkeepers—or meticulous maintenance or comfortable housing—will find this inn of a lodge, located just a football field from the ocean, a very acceptable base camp. Rooms are spartan to the point of being classic camp—summer camp, that is—they are very neat and spacious. The bathrooms are unusually large, which is ideal for those trudging back and forth to the water and sand.

Also advantageous is the spread of front lawn with lots of chairs for sitting and doing nothing, or for meeting the other guests and exchanging stories about the area's attractions. In addition to all the fascinating day trips into Delaware's past (everything in the first state is close at hand), there are summer exhibits and art classes at the Rehoboth Art League, north of town in Henlopen Acres and many happenings on the well-known Boardwalk, including regattas, band concerts and art shows. And at Convention Hall, where the August and September antique shows are held each year, there is the Miss Delaware Pageant, held at the end of June.

SEA LODGE, 15 Hickman Street, Rehoboth Beach, Delaware 19971. Telephone: (302) 227-7074. Accommodations: ten rooms; six private baths; no telephones; television in living room. Rates: inexpensive. Children permitted. No pets. No cards. Open mid-June to mid-September.

Getting There: From Rehoboth Avenue, driving toward the ocean, turn right on First Street, drive five blocks to Hickman and turn left.

History with a Capital P

WILLIAM PENN GUEST HOUSE
New Castle, Delaware

If you wonder why the name William Penn is honored in the state of Delaware, check your American history book. Or British. Penn, master of Pennsylvania, the giant colony to the north, was given this contiguous enclave by the Duke of York in 1682, eighteen years after the English captured all Dutch territory on the continent. The Dutch had been the first European settlers in Delaware, and their Fort Casimir and a couple dozen houses occupied the present site of New Castle. Penn made New Castle capital of the three Lower Counties that he annexed to his own Pennsylvania. It remained the capital until 1776, when Delaware declared its independence from both Pennsylvania and Great Britain. For the next two centuries, as capital and commerce moved elsewhere, New Castle remained virtually undisturbed, its splendid parade of buildings standing intact, its cobblestone streets untrammeled by the traffic which took to the main roads and somehow bypassed the little port.

New Castle is where William Penn first landed in the New World on October 27, 1682, along with some hundred other brave pioneers, most of them Quakers. And the house which honors his name today is where he proceeded after taking possession of his new lands—a grant from King Charles II. The ceremony was a simple one, a symbolic one: Penn was given a handful of soil, a little water, a twig and clod of turf. He then walked to the home of his host, Arnoldus De La Grange.

The humble brick farmhouse that Arnoldus built has been added to since the days of Penn but as with most homes in this most endearingly pleasant settlement, it was done with considerable style and infinite respect for the past. Today's visitor can walk the very floors with those uncommonly wide planks and sleep in the very room where the most famous Quaker spent the night. The braided rugs are new as are the furnishings, but they have been selected with history in mind and add to the feeling of being cast back in time, especially in the antique-filled living room. Innkeepers such as Mr. and Mrs. Richard Burwell, who worked the wonders of full-scale restoration in the 1960s, have special penchants for such restoration. Their proud product fits in well with the time-stood-still feeling of New Castle, especially in the Historic District bordered by Delaware Street, The Strand, Harmony and Third streets.

A Heritage Trail walking tour brochure is available at the Old Town Hall. Close to the inn and across the street from the William Penn is the Old Court House, dating from the turn of the seventeenth century, and the George Read II House, generally regarded as the finest example of late Georgian style in the country. The original courtroom of the Old Court House has been carefully restored, with interesting exhibits on the history of New Castle. Other pertinent displays are in the Amstel House, the Old Library Museum and Old Dutch House Museum. Other homes in the Historic District, most of them ringing The Green—set aside as common pasture by the first Dutch settlers— are open to the public on "A Day in Old New Castle," an annual event held the third Saturday in May. In mid-September there is an "Art on The Green" show, a month later an annual antiques show and in mid-December there are candlelight tours.

WILLIAM PENN GUEST HOUSE, 206 Delaware Street, New Castle, Delaware 19720. Telephone: (302) 328-7736. Accommodations: four rooms with twin or two double beds; shared bath; telephones and televisions in common areas. Rates: inexpensive. Inquire about children. No pets. No cards. Open all year.

Getting There: The William Penn is in the New Castle Historic District on The Green across from the Old Courthouse. Look for its modest sign, "Guests," out front.

DISTRICT OF COLUMBIA

Chaucerian Touch of Class
THE CANTERBURY
Washington, D.C.

When the nation's capital was moved from Philadelphia to the wilderness of Washington, D.C., the Secretary of the Treasury wrote to his wife that "there are, in fact, but few houses in any one place, and most of them small, miserable huts." Oliver Wolcott could not understand "how the members of Congress can possibly secure lodgings, unless they consent to live like scholars in a college, or monks in a monastery, crowded ten or twenty in one house, and utterly secluded from society."

Today the sprawling city on the Potomac has some thirty-eight thousand hotel rooms in its metropolitan area, the sixth largest concentration in the world. Some five million visitors arrive annually to stay in these hotels, adding to the city's tourism coffers over a billion dollars a year, making this the second largest industry in the District of Columbia. There are Hiltons and Holiday Inns, the massive Mayflower, the well-known Watergate (with the superlative restaurant, Jean Louis, gracing its lower depths), a Hyatt Regency on Capitol Hill, a Ritz-Carlton, a Four Seasons, and a smashing, brilliantly designed Vista International, newest of the new, with its own sensational restaurant, the American Harvest.

Through the years of traveling the Mid-Atlantic, I've stayed in most of these major hostelries, but have also found, in the midst of the city, some smaller gems. Close to the White House, across from my favorite Washington square with one of my favorite statues, "Andy" Jackson on a charging horse, is the recently refurbished Hay-Adams. Five blocks away, tucked into a triangle formed by Connecticut and Massachusetts avenues, is another favorite, The Canterbury.

170

Sandwiched into one of the finest stretches of historic homes and town houses to be found in the District, it is a century-old answer to the pessimistic prognostication of Wolcott. And it never fails to impress with its extra-step, country inn kind of care.

The doorman is always there to assist, the bell staff is efficient and ultracourteous, and there's a distinct European flair to the graciousness and quiet of the public and private rooms. Each accommodation is a suite, complete with a spacious sitting area, a wet bar, small dressing room, private bath and all the amenities, plus complimentary Continental breakfast with newspaper in the mornings and a turned-down bed with chocolate mint at night.

The furnishings are totally removed from the chain reactions of ultramod motel or hotel. I like the liberal use of flowers and the quilted, flowery patterns on the upholstery, draperies and comforters. I also like the English clubby atmosphere of their dining room, appropriately called Chaucer's. Its polished brass and dark wood decor along with its handsome table appointments, create a welcome retreat after a hard day of sightseeing, negotiating, arguing, pleading or lobbying—in this city of so much which appeals to so many.

THE CANTERBURY, 1733 N Street N.W., Washington, D.C. 20036. Telephone: (202) 393-3000. Accommodations: 99 junior suites; private baths, telephones, television (HBO). Rates: expensive. Full meal and bar service. Children and pets permitted. Cards: AE, CB, DC, MC, VISA. Open all year.

Getting There: N Street is one block south of the DuPont Circle. Drive south on Connecticut Avenue and turn left on N; the hotel is on the left side of the road.

Inn-Town Elegance
THE GEORGETOWN INN
Washington, D.C.

The number of Washington attractions—most of them free to the public—now totals over seventy. There are the dozen famous museums, the National Zoo of the Smithsonian Institution, and the incredible National Gallery with its stunning new wing, and all those monuments. But the visitor to our nation's capital should not overlook Georgetown.

Settled by the Scots seeking religious freedom, the town owed its early success to its prominent position on the Potomac River: Maryland tobacco planters carted their crop to Georgetown warehouses on the docks. The port prospered as other growers and merchants flocked to the town, building imposing residences not far from the much more humble homes of those who worked the shops and shores. Rows of sandwiched-together Victorian buildings lined the streets, while a few blocks away and hidden behind one brick wall after another, the captains of industry constructed their mansions, some in Greek Revival style, some in Queen Anne, some in Federal. Today, most of what they built in Georgetown is a National Historic District.

Among the homes to visit in the area is the Dumbarton House at 2715 Q Street N.W., built when John Adams was President and named after an ancient castle in Scotland by the émigré who first bought the acreage in the seventeenth century. Then there's the Old Stone House at 3051 M Street. Furnishings are simple, in accord with the desire to create a setting loyal to Colonial times.

Georgetown University, founded toward the end of the eighteenth century as a Roman Catholic college, is another oasis. Take a stroll through campus to study the massive Healy Hall, a brick and stone Romanesque structure designed by Smithmeyer and Pelz, the same architects responsible for the Library of Congress.

Between Georgetown University and the Old Stone House is the ideal headquarters for a visit, not to the nation's capital with all its fascinating attractions, but to this equally fascinating enclave of so many interesting shops and a tremendous concentration of restaurants, quite a few of which would be outstanding in any city. And between campus and charming yard is the Georgetown Inn, an assemblage of typically red bricks, which captures in so many ways the real spirit of the area.

Mr. Reynolds, the ever-smiling, always-accommodating doorman, has been in place close to a quarter century. The inn's restaurant was once known as *the* place to be seen in town, but the high-flying, ultra-expensive days of the Rive Gauche are long gone. An easy-to-recommend Les Ambassedeurs has taken its place. In the rooms drapes and spreads, wall colors and carpets have all been carefully coordinated and the furnishings are Georgetown Colonial.

Although not exactly a tiny little country inn tucked into some remote corner of the landscape (the feeling of country inn is heightened by the attitude of the staff and the splendidly Colonial ambiance of the private and public rooms), this hostelry is an excellent base for exploring all there is to do and see (and eat) in Georgetown.

THE GEORGETOWN INN, 1310 Wisconsin Avenue, N.W., Washington, D.C. 20007. Telephone: (202) 333-8900. Accommodations: 85 rooms, 10 suites; private baths; telephones; televisions. Rates: expensive. Full meal and bar service. Children permitted. Pets permitted but inquire ahead. Cards: AE, DC, MC, VISA. Open all year.

Getting There: The inn is 2-1/2 blocks north of M Street on the left side of Wisconsin Avenue.

Cozy Victorian Charm
THE KALORAMA GUEST HOUSE
Washington, D.C.

The Kalorama Triangle is not exactly one of the better-known regions of Washington. But for those who want to find a home away from home, who are searching for a sense of place, of friendly neighborhood feelings and highly personalized, concerned attention by a host-innkeeper, this solidly built, Victorian four-story of stone and brick is well worth taking the trouble to find.

And it's not really out in the boonies. A few minutes away is the underground Metro bringing all of the capital within reach, and just as close is Rock Creek Park, for those who want to commune with nature. For shoppers and strollers there is nearby Connecticut Avenue and Columbia Road for antiques and for various kinds of ethnic exotica— both for viewing and for consuming. And not too far is Embassy Row, with its imposing collection of diplomatic missions.

Built in the 1880s, the house is fussily maintained, furnished in period pieces and color-coordinated spreads and hangings, and accented by potted greens and flowers. There are brass beds, turn-of-the-century art on the walls, and a parlour which serves as rallying point for the complimentary Continental breakfasts and a welcome glass of sherry before the happy hearth.

THE KALORAMA GUEST HOUSE, 1854 Mintwood Place, N.W., Washington, D.C. 20009. Telephone: (202) 667-6369. Accommodations: six rooms; two share baths, all others with private baths; telephones; televisions. Rates: inexpensive, includes Continental breakfast. Children permitted. No pets. Cards: AE, MC. Open all year.

Getting There: Take Connecticut Avenue north a half dozen blocks from Du Pont Circle and turn right on Kalorama, proceeding two blocks to 19th Street; turn left one block to Mintwood and turn right again.

Boon for History Buffs
TABARD INN
Washington, D.C.

The inn itself is only now entering its sixth decade of life as a hostelry, but its origins to back to the end of the nineteenth century and the energies of three different individuals who were successful enough to erect magnificent town houses. The name, however, is far older. As any student of early English literature is aware, the Tabard Inn was made famous by Chaucer and was located in London's Southwark section, which was destroyed by fire in 1676.

The first of this trio of buildings was converted to inn by an indefatigable lady from South Carolina, Marie Willoughby Rogers, who ran the inn until her death in 1970. This center building, the main structure at number 1739 was designed in 1900 by the Washington firm of Hornblower and Marshall for a marine colonel and reflects a greatly restrained style, fronted by a flat facade and bas relief brickwork. When Mrs. Rogers converted it to inn, it was known as the Lippitt Mansion, named for its owner at the time, U.S. Senator Henry J. Lippitt, a textile millionaire from Rhode Island.

In 1928 the adjoining home at number 1741 was added to the inn: an 1888 townhouse built for the registrar general of the Daughters of the American Revolution. In 1936 number 1737, the most outspokenly Victorian of the three, was purchased as the final addition. It was designed by Washington architect T.F. Schneider in 1887. Several other homes on the street also came off his drawing boards—Numbers 1752, 1754 amd 1847—and over on Q Street in the 1700 block he designed in a strictly Romanesque Revival style. His Cairo Hotel (now converted to condominiums and the tallest privately owned structure in the capital) at 1615 Q Street reflects still another style for Schneider—East Indian.

The Tabard Inn today provides a special, simple setting to study all this history. The rooms are not elaborately furnished, many share baths, and there are few of the modern amenities one comes to expect these days. But the sense of history is certainly there. And I like that comfortable dining room overlooking the small garden, but if the food is not up to the high standards found at far higher prices elsewhere in town, the tourist can find that elsewhere—starting across the street where the Iron Gate Inn restaurant provides its own kind of vibrant history.

TABARD INN, 1739 N Street, N.W. Washington, D.C. 20036. Telephone: (202) 785-1277. Accommodations: 40 rooms; 20 with private baths; no telephones; no televisions except in common room. Rates: inexpensive to moderate, includes complimentary breakfast. Children permitted. No pets. Open all year.

Getting There: The Tabard Inn is two doors from the Canterbury.

INDEX

Hickory Bridge Farm, 102
Historic 1725 Witmer's Tavern, 86–87
Historic Strasburg Inn, 91–92
Inn at Phillips Mill, 51
Inn at Starlight Lake, The, 70–72
Joseph Ambler Inn, 54–56
Kane Manor Country Inn, 107–09
Longwood Inn, 58–59
Maple Lane Farm Guest House, 90
Mendenhall Inn, 57
Mountain House, The, 62–64
Mount Summit Inn, 113–14
Overlook Inn, 65–66
Penn Wells Hotel, 78–80
Pine Barn Inn, 81–82
Pine Knob, 64–65
Pump House Inn, 67
Riegelsville Hotel, 41
Settler's Inn, 69–70
1740 House, 46
Sign of the Sorrel Horse, 38–39
Smithton Inn, 85–86
Society Hill Hotel, 56–57
Spring House, The, 98–100
Sterling Inn, 68
Strasburg Village Inn, 92–93
Tavern Lodge, The, 110–11
Tulpehocken Manor Inn and Plantation, 83–85
Victorian Inn, 76–77
Wedgwood Inn, The, 49–50
Williamston Inn, 75
Willows, The, 109–10

INDEX TO LOCATIONS

INNS WITH BOATING FACILITIES

MARYLAND
Gibson's Lodgings, 135–36
Harrison's Chesapeake House, 148–49
Inn at Mitchell House, The, 137–38
Pasadena, The, 147
Tilghman Inn, 149–50

PENNSYLVANIA
Inn at Starlight Lake, The, 70–72
Sterling Inn, 68

NEW JERSEY
Molly Pitcher Inn, 25–26

INNS NEAR SKI AREAS

PENNSYLVANIA
Cedar Run Inn, 80 –81
Eagles Mere Inn, 77–78
Inn at Starlight Lake, The, 70–72
Kane Manor Country Inn, 107–9

CHILDREN WELCOME

DELAWARE
Corner Cupboard Inn, The, 161–63
Gladstone Inn, 164–65
Sea Lodge, 167

DISTRICT OF COLUMBIA
Canterbury, The, 170–71
Georgetown Inn, The, 172–73
Kalorama Guest House, The, 173–74
Tabard Inn, 174–75

MARYLAND
Admiral Fell Inn, 132–33
Bed and Board at Tran Crossing, 124–25
Casselman Inn, The, 115–16
Colonial Manor, 117–18
Gibson's Lodgings, 135–36
Harrison's Chesapeake House, 148–49
Inn at Antietam, 121–23
Inn at Perry Cabin, The, 144–45
Kemp House Inn, 146
Maryland Inn, 133–34
Nanticoke Manor House, 153–55
Pasadena, The, 147
Tidewater Inn, The, 142–43

Tilghman Inn, 149–50
Washington Hotel, 155–57

NEW JERSEY
Ashling Cottage, 23–25
Chalfonte, The, 13–14
Molly Pitcher Inn, 25–26
Nassau Inn, The, 29–31
Old Mill Inn, 28–29
Publick House, 27–28

PENNSYLVANIA
Allenberry Resort Inn and Playhouse, 101
Cedar Run Inn, 80–81
Century Inn, 111–13
Coachaus, 40
Coventry Forge Inn, 61
Doylestown Inn, 53–54
Eagles Mere Inn, 77–78
Fiarfield Inn, 103–4
General Sutter Inn, 93–95
Golden Pheasant Inn, 43
Greystone Motor Lodge, 88–89
Hickory Bridge Farm, 102
Historic 1725 Witmer's Tavern, 86–87
Historic Strasburg Inn, 91–92
Inn at Phillips Mill, 51
Inn at Starlight Lake, The, 70–72
Kane Manor Country Inn, 107–9
Longwood Inn, 58–59
Maple Lane Farm Guest House, 90
Mendenhall Inn, 57
Mount Summit Inn, 113–14
Mountain House, The, 62–64
Penn Wells Hotel, 78–80
Pine Barn Inn, 81–82
Pine Knob, 64–65
Pump House Inn, 67
Riegelsville Hotel, 41
Settler's Inn, 69–70
1740 House, 46
Smithton Inn, 85–86
Society Hill Hotel, 56–57
Spring House, The, 98–100
Sterling Inn, 68
Strasburg Village Inn, 92–93
Tavern Lodge, The, 110–11
Tulpehocken Manor Inn and Plantation, 83–85
Wedgwood Inn, The, 49–50
Williamston Inn, 75
Willows, The, 109–10

PETS ALLOWED

DELAWARE
Corner Cupboard Inn, The, 161–63

DISTRICT OF COLUMBIA
Canterbury, The, 170–71
Georgetown Inn, The, 172–73

PENNSYLVANIA
Allenberry Resort Inn and Playhouse, 101
Coachaus, 40
Fairfield Inn, 103–4
Historic Strasburg Inn, 91–92
Mount Summit Inn, 113–14
Penn Wells Hotel, 78–80
Pine Barn Inn, 81–82

101 COUNTRY INNS BOOKS

Country Inns of the Southwest $7.95
Country Inns of the Far West: California $7.95
Country Inns of the Far West: Pacific Northwest $7.95
Country Inns of New England $7.95
Country Inns of New York State $7.95
Country Inns of the Mid-Atlantic $7.95
Country Inns of the Old South $7.95
Country Inns of the Great Lakes $4.95
Country Inns Cookery $6.95
Bread and Breakfast $7.95
So You Want to Be an Innkeeper $10.95

If you cannot find these books in your local bookstore,
they may be ordered from the publisher:
101 Productions, 834 Mission Street, San Francisco CA 94103
Please add $1.00 per copy for postage and handling.
California residents add sales tax.

TO ORDER: Indicate quantity for each title above and fill in form below.
Send with check or money order to 101 Productions.

NAME _____

ADDRESS _____

CITY_____ STATE_____ ZIP_____

BIOGRAPHICAL NOTES

ROBERT W. TOLF is the dean of Southern restaurant critics and an internationally known writer. He is a tireless traveler and a most prolific author, now producing three to four books a year, including the most recent *Discover Florida: A Guide to the Unique Sites and Sights* (Manatee); *Addison Mizner: Architect to the Affluent* (Gale Graphics); *Florida Restaurant Guide, Gold Coast and Tampa Bay editions* (Buchan Publications): *Country Inns of the Old South* and *Country Inns of New York State* (101 Productions). A graduate of Harvard with a Ph.D. from the University of Rochester, Tolf settled in Florida in 1971 after a distinguished career in the foreign service, posted to Europe, but returning regularly to live and travel in the areas covered in this book. He is an editor of *Florida Trend* magazine and his restaurant reviews, travel, and "Good Life" columns appear regularly in the Fort Lauderdale *News/Sun-Sentinel.* A former Senior Research Fellow of the Hoover Institution on War, Revolution and Peace, Tolf is also the author of *The Russian Rockefellers: The Saga of the Nobel Family and the Russian Oil Industry,* which won a Thomas Newcomen award in 1980 as one of the best three books on business history published in this country during the preceding three years.

ROY KILLEEN, who created the drawings for this book, is an architect, formerly with Anshen and Allen of San Francisco. He has also designed 101 Productions' Mini-Mansion series of historical architectural models and illustrated most of the other books in the Country Inns series, as well as a number of other 101 books.